The Alchemy *of* Teaching

The Alchemy of Teaching

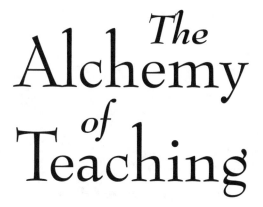

The Transformation of Lives

Jeremiah Conway

SENTIENT PUBLICATIONS

First Sentient Publications edition 2013
Copyright © 2013 by Jeremiah Conway

A paperback original

Cover design by Kim Johansen, Black Dog Design, www.blackdogdesign.com
Book design by Timm Bryson

Library of Congress Cataloging-in-Publication Data

Conway, Jeremiah Patrick.
The alchemy of teaching : the transformation of lives / Jeremiah Conway.
    p. cm.
ISBN 978-1-59181-181-7
1. College teachers--United States--Anecdotes. I. Title.
LB2331.C645 2012
378.125--dc23
                            2012026768

Printed in the United States of America

10 9 8 7 6 5 4 3 2 1

SENTIENT PUBLICATIONS
A Limited Liability Company
1113 Spruce Street
Boulder, CO 80302
www.sentientpublications.com

SAINT FRANCIS AND THE SOW

The bud
stands for all things,
even for those things that don't flower,
for everything flowers, from within, of self-blessing;
though sometimes it is necessary
to reteach a thing its loveliness,
to put a hand on its brow
of the flower
and retell it in words and in touch
it is lovely
until it flowers again from within, of self-blessing; . . .

—GALWAY KINNELL

Contents

Acknowledgments

I have been fortunate in knowing some very fine teachers throughout my life. Some had letters after their name, others did not. All of them, however, were educators in the sense of shaping my awareness through interaction with their own. It's hard to imagine this book apart from their care and example: Elizabeth Sewell; Timothy Healy, S. J.; Gerald Quinn; Anthony Sirignano; Karsten Harries; John Smith; William Gavin; Gloria Duclos; Wanda Whitten; Willard Callender; Michael LaCombe; Leonard Shedletsky; Thomas Downey; Trudy Conway; and Gertrude and Jeremiah Conway, my parents. These pages are a way of saying thanks to some and, for others, laying wreath in memory.

To Nazaré, Brendan, and Patrick (my wife and sons): your gift goes beyond teaching. It concerns companionship of the heart. For your kindness and understanding, humor and playfulness (I'll skip the teasing), for your constant hand, the words of Rilke are surely my own: "How shall I withhold my soul so that it does not touch on yours?"

Finally, a word of thanks to my students: As stories in this book attest, you (not all, but many) sustain me as a teacher. I admire your hunger to grow, your willingness to take material into your lives and be changed by it. In tough times, you are a source of hope.

Special thanks to Jamie Barilone for her contributions to the *Reading Group Guide* and to the University of Southern Maine for a sabbatical to complete the work.

Introduction

❧

I REMEMBER THE MOMENT WHEN THE IDEA OF THIS book first struck me. I was visiting my sister, who teaches at a university in Maryland. One afternoon, while she was attending a faculty meeting and I waited in her office, I started to look over her artifacts—those pictures, plaques, and knick-knacks with which we surround ourselves, making a workplace our own. Frequently, these items offer insight into a person's life and work. In my sister's case, what drew my attention was a small print tacked onto her office door of a painting by the famous sixteenth-century Dutch master, Pieter Bruegel: *Landscape with the Fall of Icarus*[1]

Although the print was one of many postings on the door, I knew that it was special. Perhaps it was how she had centered it or grouped other items around it. Perhaps it was that special

intuition that surfaces now and then when you know a person well. Whatever the explanation, I knew that it wasn't just another piece of office memorabilia. It was more like a crest or symbolic entrance into a teacher's life. For the next hour or so, I studied that print and wondered why it was there. When my sister returned our conversation shifted to other topics, and I never got to ask her about it. Also, I had enjoyed my ruminations and wanted to puzzle out its meaning for myself. So it has been. Despite time and distance, my thoughts have continued to return to the print, finding it more and more intriguing. Musings of this sort rarely end in definite answers, but one conclusion I have reached is that the picture is perfectly positioned on the door of a teacher, and I have come to understand some of the reasons why. Because these reasons have everything to do with the substance of this book, let me explain.

At first glance, it's hard to figure out what the painting has to do with the fall of Icarus. The foreground is dominated by a series of hillsides intersecting at different angles. On one, a farmer and his ox plow a field. On another, a shepherd, dog at his side, tends a flock of sheep. In the lower right-hand corner, a fisherman busily casts lines. The hillsides overlook a large body of water, through which several ships are sailing. Most prominent among these is a galleon on its way out to sea, canvases and banners billowing. Lost in the midst of this vast landscape and the bustle of figures intent on their work are two tiny legs aflutter in a final, desperate moment before they sink beneath the waves. All one sees of Icarus is that fleeting glimpse of frantic limbs just before they vanish. He appears in the painting as barely a blip on the horizon, his death hardly a ripple on the ocean's surface.

According to mythology, Icarus, along with his father, Daedalus, tried to escape from the Cretan tyrant King Minos by
making wings of feathers glued together with wax. The scheme
worked until Icarus soared too high and the sun melted the
wax, plunging him into the sea. The myth is a story of transformation: the human endeavor to overcome what imprisons
us, the courageous flight to freedom, the overlooking of limits,
and the terrible plummet we risk. As a myth about change, it
is unavoidably about pain—pain we flee, pain we incur and
cause, pain that can teach. But the most conspicuous element
in the painting is how the event of change is utterly neglected.
A tremendous event is taking place—literally the stuff of myth
and legend—but in the painting, those two sticks of bare leg
are the only signs of its occurrence. The mythic event is reduced to an insignificant detail on the borders of the everyday.
The painting seems organized around this disregard, a study
of human inattention to the event of change.

Bruegel's composition captures this neglect. In its series of
oddly intersecting planes and perspectives, each of the human
figures is caught up in his little corner, deeply absorbed in the
pursuit of individual livelihood. Each is preoccupied. No one
seems to notice Icarus or perhaps spares him only a fleeting
glance that quickly moves back to the work at hand. Everyone
is turned away from the event occurring in their midst. Instead,
their attention is roped to their work as tightly as the farm animals are tethered to their tasks. W. H. Auden beautifully articu-
lates the situation in a poem entitled "Musée des Beaux Arts,"
whose second stanza refers explicitly to this painting.

About suffering they were never wrong,
The Old Masters: how well they understood
Its human position; how it takes place

While someone else is eating or opening a
    window or just walking dully along;
How, when the aged are reverently, passionately waiting
For the miraculous birth, there always must be
Children who did not specially want it to happen, skating
On a pond at the edge of the wood:
They never forgot
That even the dreadful martyrdom must run its course
Anyhow in a corner, some untidy spot
Where the dogs go on with their doggy
    lives and the torturer's horse
Scratches its innocent behind on a tree.

In Brueghel's Icarus, *for instance: how everything turns away*
Quite leisurely from the disaster; the ploughman may
Have heard the splash, the forsaken cry,
But for him it was not an important failure; the sun shone
As it had to on the white legs disappearing into the green
Water; and the expensive delicate ship that must have seen
Something amazing, a boy falling out of the sky,
*Had somewhere to get to and sailed calmly on.*²

I believe that my sister had a number of reasons for having *Landscape with the Fall of Icarus* at the entrance to her office. First, she recognized that education, whatever else it may be about, is centrally about human change, the movements of the human spirit—its awesome flights and failures; its courage and pride; its struggles with suns and parents, tyrants and the deep. Knowing my sister, I understood that one of the print's messages was a plea: Don't forget this. Don't forget that, in the middle of classrooms, in the corners of libraries, in the quiet reading of a book, or in ordinary conversations, people can be immersed in events that are decisive to their lives, changes that put people at risk and demand our attention as teachers. Like Icarus, the young people we teach are flying near suns. They're dropping into oceans like comets. They're struggling to escape labyrinths. More than a few are drowning.

I suspect that a second reason why she posted the print on her door was the recognition that in education today, as in the painting, we often neglect the change occurring in our midst. Precisely where one would expect heightened awareness of the pains and triumphs of human transformation, there is often the same inattention shown by the sailors on the merchant ship or the farmer on the hillside—maybe more. The painting offers clues as to why. Like the figures tied to their jobs, students file through institutions of learning tethered to the line that education is the key to a successful financial future. Education is increasingly about jobs and careers, making a living; it has less and less to do with the making of lives—especially for the overwhelming majority of students whose ability to resist the immediacy of financial considerations grows slimmer with every loan they incur, every tuition hike.

But not only students are preoccupied with learning as the pursuit of livelihoods. To an overwhelming degree, institutions of higher education are caught up in the business of education as well. They cater to and reinforce the fixation on economic success. A clear sign of this obsession is the domination of educational language by the vocabulary of the marketplace and the fact that this language long ago ceased to raise eyebrows, much less resistance.

Don't misunderstand me. The problem is not that education helps students find useful, meaningful work. At issue is job and career preparation that fails to address with equal seriousness the development of the person. When students can go through entire semesters with professors who don't know their names, when professors are so focused on their fields and specialties that they forget they're teaching people, education has gone profoundly wrong. No wonder so many students choose courses according to the time of the day, read only the CliffsNotes, and worry about the number of credit hours that they need to complete until the yoke of education falls away.

In this sense, the print issues a warning: if educators merely instruct (that is, ply students with information and tools without paying attention to the people who will use them), then institutions of learning may succeed only in creating more clever tyrants, more aggressive Minotaurs, more cunning labyrinths. Daedalus conveyed his technical skills and knowledge to his son, but wisdom he did not impart, and, as the myth cautions, skills and information are not enough. Knowledge without personal development can be catastrophic.

There was, I believe, a final reason for the print on the door. Despite the foreground of inattention, a hidden background to both the painting and learning remains attentive and devoted to the dynamics of human change. That backdrop is the great reservoir of stories, myths, works of art, literature, and philosophy present in every culture and centrally concerned with the struggle of how best to conduct our lives. Given that these stories concern the issue of human transformation that lies at the heart of education, the place of such stories is central to the context of learning. In putting that Bruegel print on her door, my sister knew this. The painting portrays our blindness to the event of human change, but it does so by way of remembering the myth of Icarus' fall. The figures in it might be oblivious to the youngster drowning, but the myth and painting are not. With a deft stroke, Bruegel portrays both the neglect of human change and a path to its repair.

I may be wrong about why my sister posted the print. In some ways, it doesn't matter. It riveted me (and my sister, I'll wager) for what it says about teaching, which brings me to my purpose in writing this book. This is a book about teaching. It's not, however, about tips, techniques, or new strategies regarding how to educate. It offers no plan for educational transformation, innovation, or reform. Instead of providing some theoretical model of what education should be, it redirects attention to the actual experience of teaching—in particular, to those events of human change that education both engenders and witnesses. It focuses on the process that Icarus undergoes. Nothing in teaching, I believe, is more luminous and messy than these events: luminous in the way they capture the fundamental nature of teaching, messy in that events of change are often complex, painful, and disruptive of plans.

This book focuses on incidents of human transformation that I have witnessed and in which, as a teacher, I have shared. It relates occasions wherein such experiences were, for me, vivid, palpable, and arresting. Teachers know these occurrences. Listen to educators discuss their work for any length of time, and the talk unerringly turns and returns to student growth and change. Nevertheless, the connection between teaching and human change is often pushed to the side, neglected in the routines of daily life. It can also be administrated into something peripheral. In such ways, one of the key purposes of education is subverted and left for a commencement piety.

My sense is that we educators often find ourselves so knee-deep in recommendations and mandates, plans and proposals, rubrics and benchmarks that the connection between teaching and human metamorphosis is easy to overlook, take for granted, and depreciate. This neglect has consequences—the most serious of which is that the heavily regulated environment that characterizes today's schools can obscure, even destroy, that love of teaching without which no program, proposal, or policy can succeed. Teaching is an act of service, and service cannot be sustained without resentment unless there is deepening awareness of what factors make such desire to serve possible. Disconnect teachers from human transformation, and the love of teaching diminishes.

It's possible to dismiss stories about human transformation as merely anecdotal, lacking the generality of theory and the weight of carefully assembled facts. But, although theory and data certainly have their place, I am convinced that stories—well-told stories at least—are necessary to unearth and understand the dynamics, temporal and emotional layering, and interpersonal thickness of lived experience. The connection between stories and human change runs even deeper, however. Not only can stories articulate change, they are also vehicles for it. If we stop to listen to educators talk about their lives, it is immediately apparent how the stories they tell and retell have shaped those lives. Leading students (and ourselves as teachers) to pay attention to the stories we inhabit, to consider the possibility of alternative stories, to build upon or let go of the tales to which we are attached—these factors are critical to the possibility of human change. Lives are formed and informed through the telling of stories. The same, I believe, is true of teaching.

Perhaps an example from my own experience will illustrate my point. I went into college teaching without a single course in educational theory or practice (a fact of which I am not proud and which still leaves me scratching my head). Instead, I had to learn on the fly, which is to say through repeated trial and considerable error. If pressed to identify one factor that helped me as a teacher, I'd have to say that it was the company, early on in my career, of a group of senior colleagues who cared about teaching and talked willingly about their experiences. They had keen eyes for the humor in teaching. Many had overcome the need to appear impressive. They paid attention to their students and quietly recognized, more in deed than word, the importance of the educative act. They let me peer into their treatment of texts, issues, and classroom dilemmas. They admitted me to their struggles.

We talked in bustling cafeterias and cluttered offices. Unlike those in formal academic settings (where professional armor is thick, and no one seems to produce anything but brilliance), these informal conversations had the give and take, the doubts and playful teasing, the leisure and honesty of good talk. I could witness the pleasure of colleagues when their teaching succeeded, track their doggedness and frustrations, and sense their commitment to connecting material with young lives. This fellowship, built on sharing stories about teaching, sustained and nourished me. One motivation for these pages is the hope that my own stories of teaching might provide something of the same for others.

The incidents in this book awakened me to the enormity of the educative act, the ways in which teaching intersects with lives. They concern experiences that whispered to me, even at the time they occurred, "Don't forget this." But time passes, and events of human change are swept along in the daily stream of other activities and responsibilities. So much of what is luminous in teaching is never recorded. So many memories remain private, unshared, submerged in that ancient River of Forgetfulness that flows through all our lives.

In short, the human transformations occurring at the very center of teaching are liable to slip like water through our fingers. The consequences of this forgetfulness are numerous and substantial. For instance, the "literature" of education tends to be dominated not by literature in the sense of stories, but by factual reports and theoretical models that pay no heed to the personal. The more that stories of change go unspoken, the harder it becomes to study such events, to examine them in greater depth, to think about what elements enable and obstruct their occurrence. Teaching becomes more a matter of instruction than the engagement with lives, love of teaching an endangered species.

I'll end back at the beginning. When I first started teaching, I used to start every class with an invocation. The practice barely lasted a year and (though I wouldn't admit it at the time) had as much to do with working off nervousness as with recalling classes to a shared educational purpose. I look back at the invocation now and smile at both my earnestness and my students' patience:

> *Let us be mindful of who we are,*
> *Our poverty and our richness,*
> *And our search for what is beyond us.*
> *Remembering this, let us truly teach one another.*

However stilted the words sound to me now, this summons to mindfulness was my less colorful version of the Bruegel print. Even then, it summarized the basic concerns of this book: Be mindful of the educative act; acknowledge its snafus and successes and let them be instructive; stay close to those dimensions of teaching—wonder, passion, care—that move us beyond ourselves and are irreducible to technique. I stood before those classes very green, but I already knew the central conviction of these pages: teaching is a privilege, and lives are at stake in it.

ONE

Emma's Cave

LIKE EVERYTHING ELSE, TEACHING CAN BECOME ROU-
tine—not necessarily dull or unpleasant, but remarkably un-
remarkable. From a distance, whole semesters can seem but
blurs of activity. Perhaps this is why educators treasure certain moments when a reawakening to the fierce potential of
education emerges from the fog of the commonplace. In *The
Brothers Karamazov*, Dostoevsky writes about how the presence of even one good memory preserved from childhood can
protect and sustain a life.[3] The same, I have learned, is true of
teaching.

But instances of good teaching don't come labeled for easy
identification. They don't announce themselves, in my experience at least, to smiles of self-satisfaction and surrounding
nods of approval. Quite the contrary, moments of real teaching often resemble debacles, especially when gauged from

the perspective of everyday routine. Nor are these moments attributable to the usual suspects of scholarly expertise and pedagogical technique. These factors may be present and necessary, but they are insufficient. The experiences to which I refer spring from deeper sources.

ⳁ

It was an overcast, late fall afternoon, and I was shaking a leg across campus to avoid being late for class. My destination was a small seminar classroom at the edge of campus. We were reading a text that I had taught many times—Plato's *Republic*—as part of an interdisciplinary course in a small Honors Program at a state university.[4] The focus that afternoon was on the famous myth of the cave at the beginning of Book Seven. It's a philosophical gem, accessible and provocative, a staple of the philosophical toolbox. Students enjoy unpacking its imagery, and the labor of doing so often helps them come to grips with the structure of the *Republic* as a whole. I went to class anticipating smooth pedagogical spelunking.

My habit was to work at the myth on two levels: to examine its images in terms of the surrounding text of the *Republic* and to interpret those images against the grain of our own lives. In the myth, Socrates presents an extended image of "how education—or the lack of it—affects our nature" (514a). He asks the bright, young Glaucon to picture an underground cave where people sit, shackled at their necks and legs, such that they are confined to the same spot and can see only what is directly in front of them. It's a haunting tale, suggesting that in our ordinary lives, we start from the position of slaves whose vision is dominated by shadows cast upon the wall of the culture we inhabit—shades manipulated by figures behind our backs that we mistake for reality.

The class was working through familiar connections—how the prisoners in the myth resemble other characters in the *Republic* who are locked into stock Athenian notions of justice, how the release of the prisoners' shackles coincides with the stunned realization, prompted by Socrates' questions, of their own ignorance. We were only just starting. Given that some details of the myth will figure later in the story, let me cite a few of Socrates' further instructions for imagining his cave:

> Next, I said, compare the effect of education and the lack of it upon our human nature to a situation like this: imagine men to be living in an underground cave-like dwelling place, which has a way up to the light along its whole width, but the entrance is a long way up. The men have been there from childhood, with their neck and legs in fetters, so that they remain in the same place and can only see ahead of them, as their bonds prevent them from turning their heads. Light is provided by a fire burning some way behind and above them. Between the fire and the prisoners, some way behind them and on a higher ground, there is a path across the cave and along this a low wall has been built, like the screen at a puppet show in front of the performers who show their puppets above it.
>
> [Glaucon] I see it.
>
> [Socrates] See then also men carrying along that wall, so that they overtop it, all kinds of artifacts, statues of men, reproductions of other animals in stone or wood fashioned in all sorts of way, and, as is likely, some of the carriers are talking while others are silent.

[Glaucon] This is a strange picture, and strange prisoners.
[Socrates] They are like us, I said[5] (514a-515a).

The class was relatively small—thirteen students fairly
evenly divided in terms of gender and diverse in age. Most
had decent writing abilities (a fact that, even for an Honors
Program, was noteworthy). Even more conspicuous was their
interest in pushing themselves; they seemed hungry for learning (or at least achieving). Most took their studies seriously
and were willing to work. They also seemed to enjoy each
other's company. In short, a good class.

The range of their backgrounds was striking as well, con-
firming my sense that classrooms, like bars, are among the few
public places where we rub elbows with people whose conversation we might otherwise miss or avoid. Seated around the
square seminar table were an enlisted serviceman in the Navy,
preparing to ship overseas; a former monk, who, ten years
before, had left the Franciscans to marry and raise a family;
and the host of an alternative rock radio program. A hand-
ful of students were straight out of high school. Although
bright, they seemed to teeter acrobatically between energetic
highs and catatonic sleep deprivation. One woman provided
our dash of local color: purple hair, red-studded choker, and
gleaming lip ring. Another student, slightly older, had transferred to the university from a prestigious private college in
the Northeast. She was the most academically gifted of the
group, a sponge for secondary literature about the texts we
were reading, who asked tough, frank questions. She would
stand out in any course.

Her name was Emma.[6] I found her face striking: beautiful
skin, dark hair, intense eyes. There was a sharp angularity

to her features, mirroring, it seemed to me, the acuity of her intellect. She was painfully thin (a judgment that probably says more about me), and her leanness extended to her speech and thinking: crisp, pared, controlled. She seemed not to suffer fools easily, could be hard on her classmates, and was persistent about receiving what she considered adequate responses.

The class was proceeding uneventfully—the usual back and forth about the reading, and I was pushing students about the imagery, hoping that they would recognize the details' richness of suggestion. Why have the prisoners shackled by chains, rather than ropes? What is the odd wall at the prisoners' backs? Who are the concealed "puppeteers" walking upon it? The last question drew a heated response from Emma, who said that she didn't understand why it was important to pin down who was walking across the wall. Socrates left the figures nameless, so why not take our cue from him and leave it at that? I muttered something about my suspicion that, although she was right that the figures are nameless, they occupy a particular functional role in the allegory and that by specifying this function, we might decipher the kinds of people they represent.

Emma wasn't buying any of this response and seemed exasperated. "I don't see why we need to name who they are." She then quoted a footnote by the text's translator, G.M.A. Grube: "A Platonic myth or parable, like a Homeric simile, is often elaborated in considerable detail. These contribute to the vividness of the picture but often have no other function, and it is a mistake to look for any symbolic meaning in them."[7]

Typical Emma to come out swinging, proposing a duel between myself and a noted classicist. I tried to make light of the objection: "When Grube gets to class, we can ask him his reasons for such confident assertions about how we should interpret the text."

I don't recall her response, but I do remember that she let us know how she was also bothered by several remarks of her classmates, who attributed a sinister motive to the men casting and controlling the shadows on the cave's wall. Sensing an impasse, I turned to other students who had their hands raised.

As conversation with them proceeded, I noticed from the corner of my eye that Emma's face was scrunching up. Her eyebrows were knitting, and a closed look of disagreement, even anger—one I hadn't seen before—was taking over her face. Seated almost directly opposite her, I found myself glancing rapidly and repeatedly across the table at her while the class continued. Soon her face registered unmistakable pain. Her classmates began to notice. Furtive glances shot back and forth. Even for the attention-challenged, a "situation" had broken out that was too obvious to ignore; an elephant was center stage in the room and, try as we might to avoid it, its presence began to outweigh and crowd out everything else. Talk stopped.

After several moments of silence (none of us knowing what to say), I leaned toward the young woman. "Emma, are you all right?"

She remained silent, but her face knotted further. Slowly, she began to cry. The crying intensified. No longer a sniffle, it was a low, wrenching sob. I was at a complete loss. I didn't know what had provoked her reaction or how I might help her. More silence. I let it continue. Eventually, faced with such palpable pain, I felt that I had to say something. "I hope I (or we) haven't done anything to offend you, Emma. No one intended to hurt."

This weak statement, more polite than helpful, was all I could think to say. I followed up this response with a plea for understanding: "Could you tell us what's the matter?

She was still crying; words came out, but they were broken, blurted, random. They surfaced in loose strings: "Sometimes I come out of this class and I'm so frustrated. I don't know. I try and try and still don't get anywhere. My head hurts, and still I'm missing it. It's so frustrating. This class."

She grew quieter. There were long breaths, and the sobbing slowly ceased. Finally, in a low voice—almost as a comment to herself—she ended, "Maybe it's appropriate, given what we're reading." She was looking directly at me with a sad, lost gaze. "Maybe it's appropriate."

The comments sat there in the midst of the class. After initial fears that her crying was an outburst of bitter disappointment with me as teacher, I sensed something more and became quiet with her. I found myself clinging to her final comment: "Maybe it's appropriate, given what we're reading." The statement struck me as true the moment she uttered it, though I didn't know why. In the enveloping silence, a certain logic to her words slowly became apparent. The remark provided a thread that I could follow backward toward a source. I sat pulling on it.

Then it dawned on me. By now, she was wiping her tears with the side of her hand. "You know, Emma, I think you've said something important. A story like this forces us to wrack our brains about what it means, and it's not immediately clear what's significant and what's not. But the fact that we aren't sure, that we feel so very ignorant grappling with it, is a difficulty that I suspect Plato intentionally handed over to us. It's built into the very way he writes, using myth as well as argument." As had happened with Emma, something was breaking out in me. Words were streaming out. I was defending a way of teaching.

"Yes, it's frustrating not to be told what Socrates' images mean, to be asked to decipher them in the context of our lives. It's a pain to read the myth as if it's about us. But you know, Emma, I'm no longer able to teach this work simply by trying to pour information into your heads about Plato's philosophy. Doing that won't help. This is a work of great imagination; it arises not simply out of intellect, but out of the fabric of feeling and body. It isn't just a matter of strict definition, of this image meaning only that. If we're to understand such a work, we must enter it and read it not just as a tale from way back when, but as a story about us—as Socrates says himself. It's messy." At this point, I sensed that I was professing a bit too earnestly, so I shut up.

The ensuing silence was painful for the class. One of the older students finally spoke up.

"I just want to say, Emma, that your comments have been very important to me in this course. You've added a lot."

Others jumped in, adding comments along similar lines. It was touching to see. Knowing neither the source nor the import of her emotive reaction, they were reassuring the young woman that they appreciated her contributions. Emma didn't react.

We continued to sit silently. With nothing more to say, I sought to end the class a couple of minutes early. My head hurt, more from exhaustion than fear about my teaching. I wasn't sure what had taken place. Had this been a "teachable moment?" It bore an uneasy but closer resemblance to a disaster. I didn't know which I had witnessed, and I had no script to follow. Students hurriedly packed their books. One woman (she of the purple hair and lip ring) passed a folded note, scribbled on yellow legal paper, to Emma. We made for the exit and the fresh air of the night.

The next morning, I decided to call Emma at home. She answered and, in response to my request for better understanding, said that she preferred not to speak about the incident on the phone and asked if we could meet at my office in the afternoon. I agreed.

She arrived right on time, looking and sounding considerably better than she had the day before. The painful grimace was gone. Not wishing further awkwardness, I got straight to the point: "Emma, could you help me understand what happened yesterday? What was wrong? Why were you crying?"

She seemed to gather herself to answer, took a deep breath, and began: "You know, Professor, I came here from Williams College. I met a lot of very intelligent, ambitious students there, yet so many of them were focused on"—she waited for the right word—"results. We complained about the number of pages we had to read and the papers we had to write, but the game, yes, that's the word, was to get through the stuff and move on. We did it extremely well. But after a while, I found that a hard shell of efficiency was building up that nothing much could pierce. Read and process; read and process. Move ahead.

"When you asked us to introduce ourselves at our first class, I said that I had transferred because, after 9/11, something had happened to me. Those events shook me. I wasn't myself for some time; I don't know whether I can say why. The attacks weren't my reason for transferring, but they forced me to look at something in other students and in myself. Little by little, I grew disturbed by the distance between what we were studying and our selves. We weren't really being touched by much, if anything, in classes. The material didn't really matter to us as people or, if it did, only very rarely. Anyway, I left. I stayed away from school for a year and then came to this university. No offense, Professor, but I didn't expect much. This is a state school. My only reason for coming was that I no longer wanted my parents to pay big bucks for what really didn't seem to matter."

I wasn't sure where the conversation was leading, but I held my tongue and let it unfold.

Emma continued, "You know, most of the things we've read this semester—Homer, Sappho, Thucydides, Aristophanes, Plato, and the tragedies—I had read already. Very little was new. I'd read the entire *Republic* in two of my courses freshman year at Williams. I entered your course convinced that I was very knowledgeable about these texts, and, in a way, I am. What I mean is that I have lots of information about them. I've read commentators and listened to professors talk about them. But this course is frustrating because you ask us to puzzle out the meaning of many small details that none of my previous instructors had ever spoken about—like the question about who's walking on the wall behind the prisoners in the cave. You asked, and I wanted to shout out: '*I don't know, and I don't care, because it's not important!*'" The words came out in a loud, surprisingly blunt voice, and she stopped, as if catching herself.

"Do you see what I mean? I came here thinking that I was going to shine. I was going to show what I knew. And what happens? You ask questions about the material that don't draw on the information I'd gotten. Sometimes I feel thoughtless, stupid. I find myself questioning what I've learned." She wiped at her welling eyes with her fingers. "But it's more than this. While I was dismissing your questions, I suddenly caught myself. I saw what I was doing, and I was ashamed."

I said that I didn't understand her last remarks. What did she mean by "catching herself," and why the shame?

The young woman paused for a moment then looked directly at me. "I caught my assumptions. I realized what I was doing: by dismissing your questions, I wanted to hold the material at arm's length, to say that seeing ourselves in the story isn't the point. I wanted questions that would show off answers I already knew. I wanted to appear bright. The tears came as I saw what I was doing. I also felt shame because I couldn't stop crying; I couldn't control myself. And I'll tell you something else: for a long time in this course, my classmates didn't impress me. They weren't as quick or articulate as those I knew at Williams. I was pretty, let's say, underwhelmed. And you know what's happened? Over the course of the semester, I started to pay attention to the connections they draw between themselves and the readings. Like Bridgett and what she said about love in the *Symposium*, and what she wanted to tell her boyfriend; and Michael's comments about the difference between fear and dread in Aeschylus' *Agamemnon*, and how he's found this difference in his own behavior." She ticked off other examples. "Do you see? They've been doing what I had complained I was missing at Williams. They've been doing what I haven't, and that makes me ashamed of myself. That's why I was crying."

I wasn't sure what to say. I was going to say that she was being too hard on herself, but I saved myself from this paternalistic flattery by the realization that this was one of those precious moments when I didn't have to say anything. I was being taught by one of my students. It was a lesson I had witnessed before, but one I find riveting each time it's delivered. Whether in dramatic or quiet, unassuming ways, students are often eloquent educators about how certain philosophical works transform lives. They remind us on occasion, and powerfully, of the reasons that drove us to learn and love these texts in the first place.

When I finally did respond, I wanted to congratulate and thank her. "Emma, I think that you said something very truthful in class when you stated that crying was somehow appropriate to the text we're trying to interpret. It's very disturbing to recognize, as Socrates claims we must, that we all start our education as prisoners at the bottom of the cave. He also makes clear in the story that it's terribly painful to reorient ourselves, to turn our eyes from the shadows toward the light. Well, for my money, you were in the midst of that painful turning yesterday. You suddenly recognized that very familiar pressure to show off knowledge, to shine for others, and it led you to dismiss questions that didn't play into it. We all have these or similar obstacles. For what it's worth, I think that your statement was acute: should we begin to understand this myth, maybe a good cry is appropriate. You found yourself a prisoner in that cave. You recognized the pull of forces that were blocking you from even caring to interpret the work in other ways. My only disagreement is with the shame you felt in crying. Sure, I understand that it's very uncomfortable to be in a room with other people and lose control. But, however uncomfortable, you shouldn't be ashamed of crying. Your shame came from sensing that your motivations were shallow and unworthy of you. Fair enough. And to be struck by and feel badly about them is part of the pain that Socrates describes in turning from the shadows to the light. It's the price of admission to what he envisions as education: the "turning around" of the soul. (518d)

Emma understood, at least I think she did. She smiled faintly. Glancing at her watch, she said that she was sorry, but she had another appointment. I chimed in that I did as well, and we could walk out together. We gathered our jackets and books and made our way to the street. I don't remember that we said anything more. I sensed we both knew that a very old story had been reenacted.

Over the course of the next several days, it was touching to witness several of Emma's classmates drop little notes or comments to me about what one of them described as Emma's "meltdown." Some were likely just curious and wanted further information; others wanted to reassure me that my teaching wasn't awful enough to warrant tears. Many were just being kind. I thanked them and told them not to worry about Emma or me, that education often happens in unexpected ways.

It's been several years since that class, yet the experience stays with me. The reason has to do with the peculiarities of memory itself. Although we speak in terms of holding memories, of retaining and gathering them, certain memories come unbidden—they hold us. They claim our attention and, without our will or permission, intrude upon us at unexpected times, as if motioning to us with a curled index finger, "Come here. You need to look at and listen to this now." They exert this hold, I think, because they concern events that stand at the edge of the ordinary and disclose possibilities that, on some level, we recognize as needing deciphering and consideration. Such memories are less about events of the past than they are intimations of the future. They hold us because they indicate points of learning, possibilities for our own growth. If this description sounds strange and quirky, consider the fact that the ancient Greeks described Mnemosyne (memory) as the mother of all the muses, the source of all human creativity, and regarded certain forms of memory as originative, having the capacity to give birth to the new.[8]

This understanding of memory leads me to consider Emma's story for implications about good teaching—allusions that we often overlook. The first is that students often don't realize their roles in and responsibility for good teaching, which educators can't produce like widgets manufactured on an assembly line. Certainly, high quality teaching demands the possession and utilization of a broad range of skills—interpretation, communication, understanding, and application—but the activity of teaching can't be reduced to a skill set that certain individuals have mastered and others haven't. Instead, good teaching is an excellence that's called forth and, hence, something for which students are at least partly responsible. It's an activity that students can invite and encourage. It arises and can be sustained only in the midst of abiding mutual respect and trust, a context of reciprocal care. When this relationship is present and intact, good teaching has a chance to happen, but when that bond is absent or broken, when student and teacher barely know and are not obliged to each other, teaching withers. As care for the other ebbs, teaching becomes an unfulfilling obligation, a "load" rather than a willed engagement of energy and inspiration. My point is that teachers must witness and receive energy from students; without that exchange, burnout holds sway. Emma's willingness to personalize the cave story, to engage it to such an extent that she allowed it to speak to her about herself, was stunning to me. It reawakened my awareness of what some students are willing to give to and for their education. Emma's thoughtfulness, her honesty and pain were—I have no stronger word—lovely, and educators must recognize and allow such loveliness if teaching is to sustain itself as a vocation.

In this situation, Emma was my teacher. More accurately, the hard and fast distinction between teacher and student dropped away; both of us were learners. She was learning something about herself and her motivations for education; I was learning how unprepared I was for an experience that's the substance of the cave story: the "turning around" of the soul. It's one thing to read about this personal, painful "turning" in a text and quite another to witness the event in class.

Emma's story also recalls me to the decisive role of imagination within education. The presence of the cave story gave her a way to imagine the dynamics of her inner life and to investigate her motivations for learning. She could consider to what extent her desires to shine and stand out were chains and how they connected to what "puppeteers" in her own life had praised and rewarded. She had an opportunity to acknowledge the pull within herself to be more than an achiever, which had already announced itself in her response to 9/11, and to anticipate the kinds of struggles that would likely occur if she lived more in accordance with this insistent draw. As for myself, without that cave story, I don't know whether I would have grasped the possibility of Emma's break*down* being a break*through*. The story offered the class more than a piece of intellectual information or argument; it afforded a way of envisioning ourselves. Speaking of the myth that he presents, Socrates comments:

> Education then is the art of doing this very thing, this turn-
> ing around, the knowledge of how the soul can most easily
> and most effectively be turned around; it is not the art of
> putting the capacity of sight into the soul; the soul possesses
> that already but it is not turned the right way or looking

where it should. This is what education has to deal with
(518d).

I don't know how many times I had read this passage prior
to that class. But witnessing what happened to Emma and
realizing how unprepared I was for it, I understood how these
words about the soul and its turning can seem incredibly remote, almost fabulous notions in the contemporary world.
They're nearly dead words, quaint relics from the dustbin of
history. And yet, by entering the moving imagery of the cave,
by melding herself with it, Emma reanimated the issue of the
soul and its orientation. Her struggle taught me that Plato's
constant work with imagination is neither incidental nor phil-
osophically secondary. We learn through question and debate,
argument and analysis, but we have profound need, as well,
for images of life by which we can envision, understand, and
assess ourselves. If, as Plato says, education concerns the re-
orientation of the soul, imagination is an indispensable means
for its engagement.

The importance of imagination is evident in the spaces
that Plato leaves open and empty for the reader's thoughts to
fill. For example, that Socrates never describes how the prisoners' shackles are removed always struck me as a strange and
serious oversight. When, as readers, we come to that crucial
moment of liberation when the prisoners finally stand up and
turn around, the text fails to provide a single word of explanation about how the fetters came off. Instead, it simply invites
us to consider the hypothetical case of what life would be
like should the restraints fall away. I had always found this
omission frustrating. As a teacher, I wanted to know more
about how the prisoners managed this all-important release
from bondage. I wasn't naïve enough to expect a step-by-step

technique, but I wanted Plato to pay greater attention to this critical moment.

After the experience with Emma, however, I realized that the text's silence on this topic is entirely appropriate. I didn't foresee the change in Emma. I don't think I, or even she, could have. Teachers can do nothing to guarantee that anyone will make that depth of connection to a story. We can't engineer such a link; at most, we can invite it. The willingness to risk interpreting oneself in terms of the myth can only be accomplished by each individual. Emma took that risk, and Plato was right not to presume to explain why it happened. Even the story of the cave suggests that although teachers can assist prisoners up the steep ascent, release of the shackles is a matter beyond any but the prisoners' control. The event of liberation—why, when, and how it takes place—is part of the inescapable mystery of teaching. The most we can do, and perhaps *should* do, is witness, honor, and remember it.

TWO

Teaching Babel

∾

THOUGH I NEVER SAW HIS HORNS, A YOUNG MAN named Darwin was one of my encounters with that fabled creature "The Student from Hell." As all teachers know, these beings come in various shapes and sizes, but their common identifying mark, carved like sixes in the skull, is the ability to turn perfectly good classes into exercises of civil torture. They may not breathe fire or pull the fingernails from their enemies, but they can transform the simplest conversations into sweaty interrogations and make teaching a sentence to hard labor.

Darwin didn't look like someone from the educational dark side. He was a clean-cut eighteen-year-old from South Paris, Maine. My first impression was of someone very young (an expanding category, I'm afraid), earnest, and articulate. He reminded me of class presidents I'd known in high school— people you admire but don't want to hang out with. When I asked students to introduce themselves in the first class, Darwin announced—without any trace of opening-day jitters—that he was a committed Christian, planned to study political science, and looked forward to a career in law. *One confident young man*, I thought, this reflection followed quickly by the suspicion that there had to be an interesting story behind the name.[9]

The course was an honors seminar, organized around two trials: of Socrates in 399 BCE and of Jesus some four hundred years later. During the first half of the course, examining the Greek context of Socrates' trial, I had no difficulties with Darwin. Quite the opposite: he was well prepared, wrote intelligent papers, and asked good questions. But as we launched into the Hebrew and Christian scriptures, the tone became testy in the educational garden. Before assigning any material, I asked students to talk about their relationships to the Bible, hoping that such a discussion might show how we are invested in this material very differently than we are in Greek tales about gods and goddesses. Zeus can engage in binges of lying, abduction, and even rape without serious protest in the classroom. But catch Yahweh in even just one act of apparent cruelty, and there ensues an immediate uproar to explain, explain away, or condemn his behavior. I always saw this inevitable verbal melee as an indication that we belong to these biblical stories in ways that we don't to other mythologies. To put the thought another way, it's difficult to recognize one's belief system as a mythology.

Responses to my question ran the gamut. Some students stated that they based their lives upon this book. Others said that they avoided the Bible with a passion, finding it strange, disconcerting, and even dangerous. Many spoke of the Bible as something from childhood, a relic of Sunday or Hebrew school, largely untouched since. Following their comments, I tried to say something about my own relation to the text: I'm not a professional scholar of this material. I lack command of its ancient languages. As an adolescent, I had struggled to reject much of what I'd been taught about these stories and had agreed to teach the Bible in this course only after begetting many reasons to the contrary and much kicking and arguing.

I told them that when I first taught this course, I spent my time exploiting every contradiction I could find—an approach that proved shallow and unsatisfying. Why teach something only to run it down? How did that method of study benefit anyone? Over time, I learned to listen better to the stories, allowing for the possibility that they had something to say to me. As I did, I increasingly had the odd sense of being read *by* them.

I had barely finished when Darwin raised his hand. "When you use the word 'stories' in reference to the scriptures, are you suggesting, Professor, that we'll be approaching the Bible as a work of literature?"

I had a sinking sense about where the question was headed. "Well, yes. Human beings authored these stories, which have plots and employ imagery, metaphor, and other literary devices. What other approach would you suggest?"

Darwin didn't hesitate. "I believe that these works are the written words of God. They make this claim themselves. If we fail to consider this possibility, then I think we're not taking them seriously."

The class had suddenly become much colder. I thanked him for his perspective but knew, even as I gave it, that my "thanks" was a way of fobbing him off. Darwin's question had the potential to open up numerous lines of inquiry, and

I failed to engage any of them by shunting his statements into a "perspective." I could have asked about the relationship between stories and what we mean by truth. Are stories any less true than other forms of communication? Are there true stories? If so, how do we recognize them? To what extent does language (our own, the authors', the translators') mediate any message—divine or otherwise—that the stories try to convey? But I didn't. I blew the opportunity out of fear that students were already drawing battle lines, and we hadn't even cracked the cover of the book.

In our next class, we began Genesis. We were considering the situation of the first couple luxuriating in a garden of delight, close to God, naked without awareness, lacking knowledge of good and evil, and surviving without work. I wondered aloud to the class whether this state of affairs sounded strange to them. Martin, our resident humorist, for whom nothing is serious except snowboarding, couldn't resist the opportunity: "No," he replied, "that's how I wake up in the dorm every weekend."

A round of audible groans issued from the class. Other students (making no apologies to Martin) suggested that Eden sounded like childhood and expulsion from paradise like becoming adults. Unlike children, adults are blessed with and burdened by moral deliberation and choice; we've tasted knowledge of good and evil. We wrestle with awareness of our own and others' sexuality. We know work and labor and are aware of time. In other words, the life forms that emerged from the garden were self-conscious human beings. With tongue only partially in cheek, I tried to summarize their points: "So, if you're right, we human beings should be cheering for the snake and Eve, hoping that they disobey God in order for us to exist."

It was only when the issue of God's punishments arose that serious disagreement broke out. Some said that it was odd of Yahweh to forbid access to moral knowledge (to eat from the tree that would impart the knowledge of good and evil) and to punish people for seeking it. Other students questioned the fairness of God's punishment; after all, prior to chomping on the apple, the original couple couldn't possibly have known the difference between right and wrong.

Darwin jumped in at this point, arguing that Adam and Eve had been told explicitly not to eat of the tree and disobeyed. "They put their desire to become godlike above the need to obey their Creator. They were punished for their pride, and justly; they put themselves before God." Darwin's way of stating his ideas so definitely tended to silence his classmates. Trying to preserve room for other interpretations, I questioned him.

"Suppose you're right, and pride was their problem, could they really have known that pride was so dangerous before eating the fruit?"

"Of course they were aware," he replied surely. "They were told explicitly that if they ate the fruit of this tree, they would die."

"Yet they don't die!" Sydney blurted.

Darwin turned to her, unfazed. "Yes, they do. They die in the sense that they lose their intimacy with Yahweh. They die in that they separate themselves from God as soon as they think they know better than their Creator."

I was struck and annoyed by the young man's certainty. His confident assertions were inhibiting some and frustrating others. Sydney, for example, was having none of Darwin's explanations.

"I don't think your punishment for pride idea is so clear. This whole business of punishments strikes me as peculiar. This God makes childbirth painful for women. He punishes people by having them work by the sweat of their brows. He exiles them from 'the garden of delight.' It's as if Yahweh is making life one long punishment. What a harsh, depressing view. It doesn't make sense to me." Her cheeks and neck were flushed.

Sydney's last comments weren't addressed to anyone. Darwin, however, needed no invitation to reply. "Sure, it makes sense. Life *does* become a torment when we turn away from God's commands."

Sydney shot back, her voice rising, "You're preaching, Darwin, and I don't like it."

At this point, Sydney was ascending her own pulpit. "Face it, Darwin, there's a whole lot of blaming and punishing in this story, and women are getting the brunt of it. This divinity is one vindictive patriarch, and you refuse to recognize it. This God is one piece of work."

As accusations flew back and forth, I found myself sighing, "Welcome to Genesis." The irony in my facilitating this discussion was palpable. This confrontation wasn't dialogue; it was turf protection, artillery practice, bunker building—all rolled into one pious package. Or to steal a metaphor from the ancient Hebrews: stone by stone, walls of interpretation were rising, and I was just supplying brick for their construction.

When I glanced at my watch, I was glad to see that class was over. I left disheartened about the possibility of teaching this material. Maybe the old rule of keeping religion and politics out of bars should apply equally to classrooms. They're profoundly messy topics. We've been fed interpretations of the Bible since childhood, so it's tied up with our families, upbringing, and sense of identity. We often define ourselves in relation to it, pro or con, without having thought through its tenets for ourselves. Groups vie for correctness of understanding, with far-reaching political and social implications. Some take the stories literally. Read in this way, the Promised Land is a hunk of property, a pile of physical soil with a specific geographical location over which the devout can battle. Others approach the Bible anthropologically, as a record of ancient people's thoughts about the universe and their places within it. Understood thusly, the accounts are a collection of quaint beliefs far removed from our own convictions. The stories shrink into distant objects of scholarship—museum curios having little to do with us.

Despite my moaning and groaning about teaching the Bible, I do regard it as important. Here is the source of the beliefs that many students hold or against which they set themselves. The same is true for millions of people throughout the world. What other book has produced and continues to yield more violence and, paradoxically, solace and good works? If we avoid these narratives in classrooms, we simply drive them into vaults, where they're unexamined, or into assemblies of the like-minded, where rival interpretations are able to shun one another. These stories are too central in our lives to leave them ghettoized in churches, synagogues, and mosques. But unpacking them in diverse, secular classrooms is like asking people to sort fishing tackle—the lines are rarely straightforward; they're balled up with so much else and bristle with concealed hooks.

The disagreements in this class weren't new, but they were arising earlier than usual, and I found myself weary at the prospect of continued snipes and jabs. What to do? With no clear answer, I threw myself back into Genesis. The authors of these accounts were acute observers of human beings and their frailties. Could they have foreseen the overbearing certainty to which their stories have given rise? Were they aware of the difficulties and dangers of their words? If so, where and how did they tackle the problem?

I tried to read Genesis with fresh eyes. Before long, I found myself focusing on the beautiful and haunting tale of the Tower of Babel, and the closer I probed, the more the story seemed to speak to the difficulties surfacing in class. My hunch—and that's all it was—hinted at the story of Babel having something critical to say about reading and interpreting the Bible itself. Could this purpose account for the placement of the story within the larger narrative of Genesis—the fact that it occurs so early in the Bible, as the final piece of the general history of all humanity, and deals so centrally with the issue of language? Given that the entire story of the Tower of Babel consists of only ten sentences, let me present it here as it appears in Leon Kass' *The Beginning of Wisdom: Reading Genesis:*

And all the earth was of one language and one speech.
And as they [families of the sons of Noah] journeyed about from the east, they found a plain
 in the land of Shinar, and they settled there.
And they said, [each] man to his neighbor, "Come, let
 us bake bricks and burn them thoroughly"; and they
 had brick for stone and slime they had for mortar.
And they said, "Come, let us build for ourselves a
 city with a tower, with its top in the heavens;
  and let us make for ourselves a name, lest we be
   scattered abroad upon the face of all the earth."

But the Lord came down to see the city and the tower, which the children of man were building.
And the Lord said, "Behold, it is one people, and
they have all one language; and this they begin to do: and now nothing will be restrained
from them which they have imagined to do.
Come, let us go down and there confound their
language, that they may not understand [each]
man the language of his neighbor."
So the Lord scattered them from thence upon the face
of all the earth; and they ceased to build the city.
Therefore is the name of it called Babel, because
the Lord did there confound the language of all
the earth; and from thence did the Lord scatter them upon the face of all the earth (11:1-9).

I spent the weekend working through this story line by line
and entered the next class as if on a mission.

The operation didn't go as planned. Students quickly re-
verted to the issue of divine justice, just as they had with the
Garden of Eden story. And they saw plenty of similarities:
In both stories, people find themselves in situations that we
can scarcely imagine (an idyllic garden, a community of one
language). They somehow screw up by transgressing bound-
aries (eating the fruit, building a tower). God worries that
humans will become too powerful and banishes them. In-
trepid Sydney, no fan of Yahweh, wasted little time in entering the fray.

"So, what's wrong this time? Is there some rule against tower building? The people settle down and decide to build a city
and tower. They use their planning and skills to accomplish

something together. They make a place for themselves, and do it with their own hands. What's wrong with that?"

Darwin had his cue. "The problem again is pride, and pride gets punished. They challenge God's rule."

"Where do you find that in the text?" Claudia asked.

Darwin, answer at the ready, responded, "The story says that they build the tower to reach the heavens and to make a name for themselves. They puff themselves up, aim at being impressive. In building that enormous tower, they want to bridge the distance between heaven and Earth. They presume to reach the divine."

"What I find interesting," Claudia replied, "is that the people of Babel go on their building spree because they fear being 'scattered abroad upon the face of the earth'—which, it turns out, is exactly what God does to them. Darwin may be right about pride, but there's plenty of fear as well."

"I see your point," said Sydney, "but I don't see these emotions warranting punishment."

"I'm with Sydney," Martin chimed in. "Have any of you considered that this whole punishing God thing is just a cheesy explanation for why people are spread all over the globe, speaking different languages?"

Claudia voiced a soft, distracted "could be" but was occupied with her own suspicion. "It's interesting that the scattering that eventually happens is the result of the story's opening claim that the people of the Earth spoke one language; they had one speech. When God enters the story, the first thing he says is that, due to this shared language, 'nothing will be restrained from them which they have imagined to do.'"

"Some God," Sydney added. "He's terrified of human beings."

"Maybe with good reason," Martin offered with a smile.

I tried redirecting attention back to Claudia's comments.
"What is meant by the people of the Earth having one language and one speech?" The class went silent. *That question went over well,* I said to myself, as the thud of my discussion buster continued to reverberate. After more waiting and the same result, I decided to address my own question. "To be honest, I'm not sure. The story just gives hints—that's part of the beauty and, perhaps, point of the tale. To understand it, we have to puzzle it out for ourselves—no CliffsNotes, no glossary. To me, the story suggests that one of the characteristics we share as human beings is language. We're creatures of the word. Even in the Garden of Eden, Adam's first creative and distinctly human activity was naming the animals. From this humble beginning, we develop a linguistic world that we layer over anything that presents itself to us. We—all of us—operate in a world shaped by language and filtered by our concepts, distinctions, grammar, and reasoning. We're 'of one language' not merely in the sense of speaking one tongue, like Greek or Farsi, but by virtue of living in a world shaped by speech. We share, as well, a characteristic way of dwelling within language: Typically, we overlook the influence of language in our dealings with the world. We take language for granted and, in so doing, end up taking everything it touches for granted. We overlook the extent to which our sense of reality is a partial, filtered, imperfect grasp of what infinitely exceeds it. To be 'of one language' is to be of one mind and heart about the most fundamental aspects of living, and I'm afraid that, ordinarily, our minds and hearts are remarkably careless. We assume that we have a clue when we don't."

"If that's what being 'of one language' means," Sydney asked, "then why is Yahweh worried? If he's this big, all-knowing dude, then why should he sweat the fact that humans are careless about language?"

I looked into Sydney's clear, blue eyes and saw that she wasn't being clever or dismissive. She was genuinely puzzled. "Great question, Sydney. I'm not sure I have any answer. But a couple of things cross my mind. God could be worried that he's being sold short, like everything else, because we think our opinions adequate. Second, there are links in the Babel story between our being creatures of language and our abilities to foresee and plan, reason and make, design and build. We humans are clever makers. We have the inclination and ability to alter our world. But if we aren't careful, our building can obscure the overwhelming richness of what-is. We create, just as we speak, for many reasons: to protect ourselves, to find security, to cope with boredom, to escape death—or, to be more positive, because we're taken up in wonder and gratitude. Babel suggests that we often create from a desire to stand out, to be superior, to make a name for ourselves, a phrase that seems to combine both a concern for celebrity status and the use of language as a tool of power. We become proud of our skills, confident of our achievements, and impressed with our (so we think) self-sufficiency. We start conceiving and remaking the world according to our own imaginings—all thanks to our ability to use language to frame and order the world, which we reorganize to our design and purpose. We start to impose our order on the Earth to the point that, as Yahweh anticipates, 'now nothing will be restrained from them which they have imagined to do.'"

Claudia saw where I was going. "So, you're suggesting that building the tower is a kind of prophetic metaphor about us, about our situation. It's a critique of the world we've come to build and now inhabit. We live almost entirely within human environments. While nostalgic for nature—look at our 'wildness parks' and the potted trees that dot our malls—we increasingly live within environments that we've created: media networks, power grids, food chains, health systems, genome projects, and worldwide webs. All around the globe, we speak the same language of making the world over in the image of what we think it should be. This is our one language."

My grateful response was, "Exactly. Maybe it's only in the modern world that we're beginning to see what worried Yahweh. Maybe we're seeing more clearly that there are, or at least should be, limits to our creative power as we reach the point where we seriously debate whether we're rendering the Earth uninhabitable. We're beginning to witness that as our technological powers and ambitions grow, our destructive potential expands proportionately. Ziggurats are one thing, nuclear reactors quite another."

But Darwin wasn't through with us. "Before you continue on about Babel being an early lesson in environmentalism, I want to check an issue of translation. The first line that you've been translating as 'one language, one speech' is in my text 'one language and few words.'[11] To me, that's a significant difference."

I couldn't help but take his comment as a smirking criticism that we were trying to make sense of the story without knowledge of the original language. "I can't really say which translation is more accurate. I don't know ancient Hebrew."

"Neither do I," Darwin responded, "but I wonder whether it's really possible to teach this material without knowledge of the language."

I was stunned. *You little twerp,* I thought. His comment stung, partly because I had posed the same question to myself many times—who was I to teach the Bible? Here, however, the suspicion came from a student and in public. Darwin, I was sure, considered me an imposter. He wouldn't be satisfied unless the interpretation of the Scriptures was conducted in a church by factory-approved technicians. I tried to mask my anger with a display of expertise.

"Yes, of course, the issue of language is important and complicated. What we're reading is the product of multiple layers of translation, each with the potential of doing violence to the meaning of the original. Come to think of it, it's tough even to establish the original language of the story. Was it ancient Hebrew? Probably not. The Hebrew itself may be a retelling of an ancient Babylonian myth in Aramaic. The Aramaic text—if it ever existed—isn't available. A Chaldean version written in Akkadian is available, but it's fragmented and different from the Hebrew."

I was struggling to regain some professorial ground. The remarks came off as pedantic, which was their purpose. They bought me time. I started to calm down and decided not to engage the Fabled Creature but to move forward. "Let's take stock of what we've been saying," I suggested. "We've been pursuing the idea that the one language shared by the people of Babel is evident in their construction of a tower to the heavens and their attempt to make a name for themselves. Their shared speech is, we've been speculating, their use of language to impose their will upon the world. Before we examine God's response in the story, let's go back to Claudia's point and see if we can really appreciate the dangers in the spread of this 'language.'"

Normally laid-back Claudia seemed unable to restrain herself and responded immediately, "Well, like I said, if we constantly speak this way, we lose sight of what lies beyond our mental framework. The impulse to look at everything as a resource, as something to use, can produce enormous technological advances, but we can easily lose sight of the costs of this exploitation. We forget our dependence on everything not of our own making. We become so entranced with the desire for status and power that we forget our interconnectedness with the rest of life and our obligations to it."

Claudia was on a roll, and I had the good sense to keep quiet. "Language is our means of grasping the world," she continued. "We probably can't help it. But it becomes easy to think of things only as we conceive of them. We forget that our language and thought are very partial; they never do justice to the things we speak about. People and things shrink into our idea of them." With this observation, she seemed to have talked herself out. I waited a bit after she had stopped then posed a question to the class: "So, if Claudia is right about the dangers of 'one language,' what do you think about the Lord's response to confound their speech and scatter them? Is it cruel, misguided, or what?"

Martin was the first to speak. "If Claudia is right, I'm not sure that the scattering is a punishment in the sense of getting back at someone for some misdeed."

"What other kind of punishment is there?" Sydney asked.

Martin responded, "Sometimes punishment arises naturally. You know what I mean? Reaping what we sow. Getting what's coming to us. Seeing the consequences of our behavior. It's as if God foresees the inevitable outcomes of the project to build the tower right from the beginning."

Sydney leaned forward with a puzzled look. "I'm not sure I see what you mean."

Claudia jumped back in. "Maybe he means . . . forget it, I'll just say what I mean: The project had to fail. When our language is about power and control, and the important thing is to impose our will, it's not long before this approach to the world spawns multiple rivals, each seeking to climb to the top of the heap. Different cities construct different towers, all seeking to make a name for themselves, each trying to be more impressive than the other. The towers become immense. People see them as threatening and attack them. Even when the fighting doesn't reduce the towers to rubble, it assures that everyone is crippled. The populace is desperately poor but heavily armed; cities remain half built, with cracked arches and damaged roadways. The human landscape is a battlefield of partisan conflict. We drive each other into the ground. Yahweh, in scattering the people who built the tower, confronts them with the destructiveness of their own actions. He lets the consequences of their motives unfold into the fragmentation they harbored from the beginning."

Claudia's comments seemed to affect her classmates, who went quiet for a moment, until Martin congratulated her. "That's a depressingly cool insight, Claudia." Everyone smiled except Darwin, who sat with his hands folded in front of him, shaking his head.

"If the Lord's intervention is just playing out the consequences of pursuing power and status, then God seems pretty superfluous. He doesn't need to do or say anything. You" (and here he was looking directly at me) "seem to interpret God's words and deeds as just a clever way to illustrate a problem with technology. God becomes a figment of the human imagination, a convenient explanation for our being scattered."

"That isn't my view, Darwin, and I don't think it's Claudia's. The story does state that God acts and speaks against the Babel builders but doesn't specify the form of the Lord's language and action. Guess it depends on the meaning of God's acting and speaking. I don't hear voices from heaven, but I do believe that there's an incredibly intricate pattern of life, and when frogs start dying off, when oceans rise, when kids all over the globe aspire to be suicide bombers, these are wordless 'voices' to which we should pay very close attention. I imagine that the ancients read similar signs."

Darwin was undaunted by my sermon. "You know, when I hear you interpret this material, Professor, it always seems as if God is disappearing into something else. You don't actually believe that there was an Eden on this Earth, no exile from Paradise, no universal Flood, no Ark. You seem to regard the whole thing as an anthology of fictions, a collection of poetry. You start making God out to be some ecological warning."

I'd had it. I was tired of his putdowns and, as these biblical texts might say, my tongue was loosed upon him: "And you seem to me like someone who has shrunk God down to your orthodoxy. The only real flood for you is one you can float a boat upon. You're poetically challenged, Darwin. I think there are innumerable floods—catastrophes that don't require water. And there are arks that aren't made of planks. And the same, I suspect, applies to God. You ought to pay attention to what numerous religious mystics affirm: that the greatest obstacle to the experience of God is one's idea of god. You accuse me of wanting to reduce God to a human idea; ironically, that's the one thing to which I'm fundamentally opposed. If anything, I believe that God is the very mystery of life, beyond any and all of our ideas—the living reality of what-is, to which all our

words and ideas gesture and none exhaust. If we drew close to
it, it 'would fell us with its fragrance' and that, dear Darwin,
is from one of my poetic buddies you disparage."[12]
Darwin was equally direct. "Your idea of God as mystery
is awfully vague, Professor. It's also pretty safe; it doesn't offend anyone and demands nothing of us. Mystery doesn't impose any commandments. My life as a Christian is an effort
to identify with Christ, to make my life more like his. His
life gives me an orientation, a sense of what's important and
necessary, what to cultivate in my actions. It asks something
of me." (*Yeah, like charity of spirit*, I said under my breath.)
"Mystery doesn't commit you to anything," he concluded.
We were beyond niceties. "Darwin, you're so totally committed to your ideas that you're oblivious to anything else.
You've got me pegged to your little category of academic air-
head, and there's nothing I can say or do to escape it. And—
this is the really big 'and,' sonny—you don't know jack squat
about me."

For some reason, the earthiness, the rodeo resonance of
"jack squat" suddenly struck me as terribly funny in a conversation about divinity, and I started to laugh. Maybe it was
just exhaustion. In any case, the laugh wasn't a chuckle. It
was mirth of biblical proportions that, once underway, wasn't
stopping and simply pulled me along for the ride. Moving
from Yahweh to jack squat was just too bizarre and delightful. I laughed till I cried. Darwin, poor guy, didn't know what
to say or do. By the end, while I was wiping my cheeks, his
initial look of puzzlement had buckled, and he eked out a
smile. It had been a long, tiring class, and I was glad it ended
on a note of the ridiculous. We would have the weekend to
regroup, lick our wounds, and come together again.

On Monday, as I headed to class, I saw Darwin waiting outside the classroom. He wasn't in the morning course, so I was suspicious as I approached. "What's up?" I asked.

"I have something for you," he replied and reached into his book bag, pulling out a piece of paper.

"What's this?" Before he could answer, I recognized the withdrawal slip he was handing me. The sight of it hurt. "Oh, Darwin, I hope you're not thinking of dropping the course. Don't do it—not after all the work and effort, not now when the semester is already more than half over. Not at this point."

He saw my disappointment. "I just think it would be better," he said quietly.

Already late for class, I asked that we meet that afternoon during office hours. He hesitated but agreed.

The prospect of Darwin dropping the course bothered me all day, but I trusted that I would be able to dissuade him. I realized that I admired the young man in many ways. He believed in something and tried to be clear about it. He had the guts to stand up for his ideas, speak his mind clearly, and try to live his convictions. He took his studies seriously and was unafraid of hard work or contention. He also tested me.

By the time office hours arrived, I had rehearsed several speeches. Darwin arrived right on schedule, his withdrawal slip protruding from his fat copy of the Bible. I tried to be as conciliatory as possible. "Look, last class we both said annoying things. But we ended up having a good laugh together, and I was glad we did. I regret saying anything that might have hurt you." I was about to continue, but he cut me off.

"I wasn't hurt by anything in class."

I waited for him to say more, but he didn't, so I decided to get to the point: "Then what's with the withdrawal request? Why now?"

Darwin had the habit of sitting very upright in class and looking people in the eye; now he was bent over with elbows propped on his knees, his chin in his hands. "I just think it's for the best," he mumbled. More silence.

"Come on, Darwin, that's not an answer. I deserve more than that."

He hesitated a long time before speaking. "You remember in one of our first classes on the Bible, we spoke about the meaning of the term *religion?* You said that the word was derived from two roots: *re*, meaning 'to do again or go back,' and *legare*, meaning 'to bind,' so that the word *religion* literally means 'to bind back or bind again.'"

"Yes, that's right. Glad someone was paying attention," I replied.

He continued, "Well, what I took from that discussion is that religion involves a search for connection, for ties, and that's what my religion is for me. It's a way of gathering and sustaining bonds, of belonging. That's very important in my life. It matters."

"I agree."

Again, he stopped. I waited. Finally, he muttered, "Do you, Professor?"

"Do I what?" I asked.

"Do you really see the importance of bonds, of community?" He raised his head, bypassing any response from me. "I hope you don't mind me asking, but do you belong to a church?"

"No, I don't," I answered.

"So, where do *you* find community and connection?" he asked. "Do you find it in the university?"

I was a little taken aback by his question and took time in answering. "I find it with my family and with friends," I said.

"I find it in teaching and, yes, in pockets at the university."
My voice was trailing off, and I knew why. Community was
a tough issue for me. Aside from those early days of conversations about teaching, I had looked for it in university life but
had rarely actually found it.

Even now I see community as desperately needed in education but largely absent. Universities tout themselves as *intellectual* communities, but somehow the qualifier always strikes
me as an indication that they are more communities in the
abstract than in lived practice. In actuality, universities today
are associations of independent contractors rather than places
of real belonging. Of course, I didn't want to share any of
these thoughts with the young man before me.

Darwin seemed to sense my discomfort and spoke again,
"For me, it's different. Religion is everything in our house.
It's the glue of our family. It's what we're about. It sustains us
through tough times."

"I'm not trying to pull you away from any of that," I interjected.

"Whether you try or not," he continued, "the result is that
things come up in class that are very different from what I've
been taught. No offense, Professor, but some of what you say
seems silly to me, but other things are unsettling. I find myself
questioning. I sense bonds loosening. I don't like it."

"*You* don't like it? I asked, emphasizing the pronoun.

"Meaning what?" he shot back. I knew that I had struck a
nerve.

"I'm just wondering whether you're getting any pressure
from your parents or your minister," I replied.

"I'm not being pressured at all," he responded. "My dad's
happy that I'm at the university, even if it's secular. He knows
I'm secure in my faith."

"So, he's not urging you to drop the course?"

"No . . . not really," Darwin's words suddenly sounded shaky, and he regrouped. "Look, my dad and I talk over my work a lot, especially in this course. I don't know if I mentioned it before, but my father is a minister. He's pastor of a church up in South Paris. He's studied the Bible his entire life, reads it every night, and has some pretty definite thoughts about it."

I pushed a little further, "And what about your mom? You haven't spoken of her. What does she think?"

He turned away slightly. "I don't get to see her much," he said softly. "My parents got divorced eight years ago."

The pennies dropped from my eyes. I was beginning to understand some of the pressures upon this young man. He wasn't just interpreting an important book; he was wrestling with membership in a community of believers, negotiating his place in a family, deciding upon his relation to his father. "What does your father think about how we've approached the Bible in this course?" I asked.

His response was immediate, "He thinks you're another secular humanist."

"Do you know what he means by that?"

"He means that you're reading the Bible without commitment; you're reading without seriously considering that the Lord has addressed it to you, that if you listened carefully, it could help direct your life. He means that you're trying to live without guidance."

I smiled. "Sounds like your father knows me pretty well. What do *you* think, since *you're* the one who's taking the course?"

Darwin glanced at his watch. "I'd like to stay and talk, Professor, but I have to be going. It's a long drive back to South Paris."

"No problem," I responded, "but I'd like to talk further with you about withdrawing."

He looked at me directly and said, "I'm not going to change my mind."

"Fair enough, but there are a few things you should know: The university won't refund your tuition this late in the semester. Also, any withdrawal has to be approved by the dean, and she'll need a good reason in writing. Withdrawal for 'reasons of irreconcilable religious differences' just won't fly as a justification. Besides, I'd like you to stay in the course. Why not wait another class or two and think about what's best? Don't rush into it. I hope that you'll reconsider."

Our next class was on Exodus, which struck me as oddly appropriate. I was glad when he showed up. I had prepared the class with Darwin in mind, trying to find a way to convince him to stay. It was probably a mistake. I don't remember much class conversation, probably the result of focusing on what I wanted to say to Darwin through the text. I was pushing the idea that Exodus is a story about all of us. We all grow up in service to certain Pharaohs, and part of spiritual growth is learning how to contend with them. Liberation isn't easy. The more Moses pushes, the more the Pharaoh pushes back. The struggle resembles some titanic isometric exercise, wherein different parts of our selves pull against each other. Liberation, if and when it occurs, isn't greeted with applause and banners but with a long sojourn in the wilderness—a journey so difficult that the participants long for their former slavery in Egypt.

Darwin was silent throughout the class. Eventually, near the end, he piped up: "If I follow you, Professor, you're saying that the story of Moses' journey to the Promised Land is a metaphorical account of transformations within us. For you, there is nothing historical in this account. No Moses. No definite Promised Land. No tablets with commandments. It's just another good story."

"Yes, only your use of the word *just* bothers me. Stories are vital and unavoidable. Our lives depend on them. Our consciousness, I believe, is structured in terms of stories."

Darwin looked at me directly. "So, how do you choose which story to commit yourself to, if there's nothing outside them?"

My reply was immediate: "I didn't say that *all* we have is story. But whatever is beyond our stories, we have to make sense of within them."

"You didn't answer my question, Professor."

"I'm dancing as fast as I can, Darwin. Some stories are better than others. Some seem false or contrived. Others open new possibilities; they show us that there's more to life than we thought. Finally, though, I agree; it's very difficult to choose which story to believe, and a lot hangs upon that choice. Sometimes, when we remain unsure, all we can do is try to keep the question alive."

I was speaking just to him. I couldn't help it. I had reached the point of professing, which can become awfully close to preaching. And I was doing it for all I was worth. "One thing I'm sure of: we each have to search and choose for ourselves. If religion is a search for bonds, as we've said in previous classes, then searching makes no sense without acknowledging that we are, to a significant extent, lost. Religion makes no sense until after the expulsion from Paradise."

Darwin stopped me. "But some people enjoy being lost; they make a profession of it. They can't or won't recognize truths in the Bible." I knew that he numbered me among these lost souls, and I wanted him to say it. "Do you mean me, Darwin?"

He answered without hesitation, "That's the way I see it, Professor."

His presumption was breathtaking. I smiled and responded, "You might be surprised, my friend, about the truths I find in this book. But since you're not asking, let me tell you one. I happen to think that there *is* a central truth in the books of the Bible. I can put it this way: Like the Jews, we're often unimpressed with God's miracles. There's a tendency for us to become utterly nonplussed with life: 'So, this is life?' 'Is that all there is?' In the midst of our pleasures, we worry that they won't continue. In our activities, we find ourselves bored. In the end, we all die. Do you see what I mean? Many people experience a deep dissatisfaction with life that infiltrates even religion. You can see it in Exodus. The Hebrews tell a story of slavery and dissatisfaction, of a thankless people grumbling in the wilderness. To their credit, they have the courage to admit it. And that admission is crucial, because the search for bonds requires recognition that at an elemental depth we have become disconnected and rootless. We all have our Pharaohs and conditions of slavery, and there's no liberation without facing them—however important they are to us. Too often, we go with what's near and dear and convenient."

I looked at Darwin but had trouble reading him, other than having the fleeting sense of someone withdrawing. The shuffling of books signaled that class had ended. I felt like I had been standing on a soapbox—a difficult stance from which to teach. In fairness, I was fighting for several things and sensed that the clock was ticking. Partly, the fight was to convince Darwin to stay. It was also a fight, however strange it sounds, for the importance of classrooms as public sites of examination, as places—rare and special—dedicated to questioning, self-reflection, and dialogue. Working with the biblical material makes me especially aware of the gaps and fissures we negotiate in classrooms. The story of Babel is a meditation on this situation and, as such, has much to say about teaching generally and the Bible in particular. We are, it suggests, incredibly scattered, our tongues confused; this claim underscores why classrooms, to the extent that they *are* places to engage our differences and confusion, are so precious. Babel has implications for teaching the Bible as well, for it rules out any interpretation that presumes itself adequate, complete, or final. It rebukes all claims of dogmatism, which is why I believe that the story appears centrally in Genesis. If so, its message has been roundly missed.

Darwin never returned to class. I waited expectantly for a time, but, as days turned to weeks, I gave up. I suppose I could have called him, but I didn't know what else to say. I never signed his withdrawal form, and when I had to submit grades for the semester, I put down "incomplete," which seemed poetically accurate.

The class was different after he left. Less headaches, fewer jabs, yet less at stake somehow. His departure seemed like fitting testimony to the story of Babel. We are, indeed, scattered, our languages confused. The thin tightropes of words that we throw across our fissures are so tenuous. This fragility isn't a reason to give up but to acknowledge the chutzpah of teaching, the difficulty of its venture.

With Darwin's departure, a silence infiltrated the classroom. It felt emptier. His leaving also taught me a lesson about Students from Hell. These fabled creatures were, I had assumed, individuals who could lead teachers to abandon their stance as educators, learners who could cause them to forget themselves, to lose, however temporarily, their posture as teachers. Yet as I mulled over this thought, I recognized that the only person capable (and responsible) for such loss is oneself. Students from Hell mark my limits as a teacher. They show me where I must grow. Darwin, with his insistent certainty, his unquestioning acceptance, could press buttons in me because of struggles that I had considered buried in the past. Seeing traits in him that I had battled myself, I did what was familiar: I fought like the devil and ceased being a teacher.

Darwin taught me another lesson: I'll never use the expression Student from Hell again. As Babel teaches, we are terribly scattered, and if we withdraw from each other and retreat from classrooms, we risk being less troubled by the confusion of our tongues. We presume to know each other, yet so much escapes us.

I miss Darwin. I never found out the story behind his name.

THREE

Darcy and
the Red Sox

IT WAS A HARD NIGHT TO FORGET: THE RED SOX were on the brink of winning a World Series for the first time in eighty-six years. With three victories already in hand, a dark cloud of success loomed over New England. Hearts that had learned to accept defeat as stoically as they faced April blizzards were unsettled by the possibility of victory. As the saying goes about the Irish, Red Sox fans have "an abiding sense of tragedy that sustains [them] through temporary periods of joy."[13] Tonight, however, was different. An unnerving optimism was loose upon the land.

It would be a tough night to teach. Many of the usually baseball-capped males and more than a few women would be absent, I expected, for "circumstances beyond their control" or "family emergencies." Yet entering the classroom, I saw that the anticipated boycott had not occurred, though the faces beneath the brims were not radiating enthusiasm. Students had barely taken their seats when a hand shot up with the first question of the evening: "Can we end class early tonight?"

Uplifting start, I murmured to myself. Luckily, I had my response prepared. "We didn't end early last week and look what happened" (on the previous Wednesday, the Sox had completed an improbable, come-from-behind victory over the Yankees to make it into the World Series). I reached back for the knee-buckling curveball: "Would you really risk jinxing the streak?" Silence ensued. Finally some of "the caps" began to smile, caught between a terrible argument and an appeal to the superstitions lurking within all baseball fans. Superstition won hands down.

The class was an upper level course in "Philosophy and Literature" that examines how philosophers in different cultures and historical periods conceive the relationship between philosophy and imaginative literature. What role does imagination play in human life? How does it affect thought and behavior? What is the relation between imagination and reason? The course pairs philosophical texts with novels and poems: Plato with Homer, René Descartes with Giambattista Vico, Martha Nussbaum with Charles Dickens, Martin Heidegger with William Carlos Williams.[14]

We met Wednesdays for two and a half hours in a classroom with the institutional feel of a hospital—pastel-colored cinderblocks interrupted by blackboards and a cork message board plastered with advertisements for how students could earn big bucks in their spare time. Along another wall, radiators emitted gasps of heat loud and wheezy enough to fuel a love for the great outdoors. It's amazing that we educate people in such places—no pictures or memorable words, no plants or comfortable chairs, no whimsy or beauty. This space was so "functional" as to seem uninhabited. It bore no trace of the people within—the architectural equivalent of the message *no one lives here*.

The design was ironically appropriate to the text we would be discussing tonight: *Hard Times* by Charles Dickens. The novel begins in a classroom as bare and uninviting as the one we inhabited. The school is set in nineteenth-century industrial England in a grim little place called Coketown. Convinced that times are hard, the school has dispensed with the "fancies" of storytelling and other forms of imaginative activity for the sterner stuff of scientific fact. Students are filled with factual information and tested on their abilities to memorize and reproduce it. They learn discipline, time management, and obedience—indispensable skills in the work environment for which the school is preparing them.

I wondered whether my students (most of whom are first-generation college educated) found similarities between their situations and those of their counterparts in Coketown. What warnings had they received about hard times today? What advice had they heard about which subjects to study or avoid? What pressures were they under, such that they envisioned their education—almost without exception—in terms of career and financial success? To what extent had their schools been responsible for perpetuating the "learn to get a job" message? Had these places of learning challenged this piece of conventional wisdom or, like the school in Coketown, reinforced it?

It's a tough issue. As parents, we hope that our children will find meaningful work and careers, that they can connect their studies to long-term goals, including employment. As a teacher, however, I know that the constant drumbeat of this message contorts education into job training and pressures educational institutions into catering to this demand. Many do. Although no university would openly declare art, literature, and philosophy unnecessary frills, the hidden curriculum of many institutions (how they act versus what they say) is quite articulate: universities are job and income generators. This presupposition is carved into their very architecture. Visit any campus and look at recently constructed buildings. They'll be those most closely connected with corporate and government research interests. The likelihood of a gleaming new center for the humanities is almost (some might say completely) ludicrous.

Hard Times illustrates the consequences, personal and societal, of attempting to diminish imagination in education. It takes readers into the lives of several children, tracing their growth into young adults. Dickens shows how stunting imagination leads to serious consequences in the development of lives. Without imagination, we are prisoners of any prevailing formations of reality. We lack awareness of alternatives and fail to recognize that our sense of reality is a work of imaginative construction. We believe that we can easily separate fact from fiction, speculation, and theory. But these neat divisions oversimplify the complexity of facts. Facts don't simply appear; they show themselves within lived contexts, in relation to the questions we ask and the assumptions we make. They are inseparably connected to our understanding of the world. As the Latin root of the word *fact* (the verb *facere,* meaning "to make") shows, facts are constructed, emerging from our (unavoidably mental and emotional) engagement with our myriad environments. The idea of simply beholding facts, of objectively drawing data from sheer observation, is a pipe dream. But as imagination atrophies, we overlook its contribution to the appearance of the world. We begin to assume that facts are given, that they spring up, fully formed, like Athena emerging from the head of Zeus. We mistake *our image of reality* for reality itself.

The consequences of this mindset strike deeper still. As imagination weakens, our relationships with others harden. We become increasingly harsher, more inconsiderate and callous. Reasons for this growing insensitivity are not difficult to discover. An active imagination is necessary to enter into the lives of others. As the saying goes, we cannot understand another person without walking a mile in her shoes. Stopping to think about the claim of this proverb, we quickly realize that imagination is a required tool for donning the leather. To see *into* others, we must construe their experience, and, without imagination, such work is impossible, as the interior lives of others are unavailable to sight.

The effects of an unimaginative education spread yet further. Without awareness of others' inner lives, compassion weakens. Such sympathy presupposes awareness of suffering and, except for overt, undeniable examples of it, suffering often loves to hide. We hide pain, put on a good face, pretend that nothing is wrong. We dislike appearing weak. We must possess imagination to see into all but the most obvious examples of pain, and, to the extent that we refuse the effort, we become thoughtless and grow insensitive to any suffering not immediately apparent. We become less kind and more oblivious to each other.

The atrophy of imagination affects more than just human relationships, extending to our attachments to the inanimate world as well. Lack of imagination diminishes objects, reducing them to the obvious as the impulses of wonder, question,

62 Jeremiah Conway

and care—those forces that allow us to move beyond appearances—become flaccid and lax. These emotions, all of which require imagination, give access to the depth and girth of reality. In short, without imagination, entities petrify—in a truly ironic twist—into our image of them. Lack of imagination blinds us to its operation in our lives, with dire consequences. We lose touch with the possibility of the world appearing otherwise and the all-important awareness that there is, or could be, a compelling mystery to what-is. Objects become straightforward and uninteresting (especially in that original sense of *inter-esting*, that is, being "in the midst of"). As imagination goes unexercised, we tend to take the world for granted and grow increasingly careless with it. We fail to appreciate our involvement in how reality appears.

Dickens also shows how inattention to imagination turns school into an exercise of monotony. Students endure the tedium of committing mountains of information to memory, all the while knowing that they will jettison the crammed data as soon as the test is over. A passionate intelligence cannot take root in the transfer of information alone. The soil isn't rich enough. Without some larger sense of purpose for gathering facts, without some vision of what the knowledge of facts can allow us to accomplish, without the experience of delight and wonder in learning—all of which depend on imagination—education becomes a sentence to forced labor that all but the relentlessly ambitious or the chronically obedient refuse to tolerate. Sticks and carrots substitute for inner motivations to learn. Education becomes a joyless, externally imposed chore. As *Hard Times* illustrates, children forced to endure unimaginative education will seek escape. To use the novel's telling example, they run to peek under the flaps of circus tents, desperate for an alternative to lifeless, prepackaged learning. For the young today, the circus tents are often drugs and drunken adventures. These youths seem to be shouting in fierce abandon: "At least let me feel alive!"

Granted, education is not solely accountable for cultivating humanity, and we cannot underestimate the contributions of others in this endeavor (family, friends, media, churches, clubs, sports, etc.); nevertheless, the development of people remains one, if not *the* primary responsibility of schools. If education abdicates this task, it risks promoting a narrow intelligence in increasingly less humane creatures. Given the vast, unprecedented explosion of technological powers at our disposal, such a prospect should give us pause at the very least. As schools drive imagination out of learning, they spawn an arrogant disregard that ripples out until it encompasses our entire relation to the world. Dickens captures this point in his choice of the name Coketown for the setting of his novel. Coke is the solid residue that remains after the gases and liquid of coal have been distilled through a process of intense heat and compression. Coal, becoming coke, contracts into hard, compact, combustible pellets. The education taking place in Coketown achieves the same result in terms of people. Distilling imagination out of education produces human beings whose lives are small, hard, and combustible. Even the physical environment of Coketown, the dreary, oppressive haze that envelops it, results from the failure to imagine nature as anything other than a machine or exploitable resource. The environment mirrors the education and vice versa.

The teachers in *Hard Times*, two pathetic characters with the appropriate surnames of Gradgrind and McChokumchild, are convinced that education needs to emphasize "Facts . . . Facts . . . Facts."[15] Imagination is an unnecessary and self-indulgent frill. Ironically, their insistence on the unimportance of "fancy" (their dismissive term for imagination) underscores the unattended use of imagery in their supposed imageless educational program. They conceive of education as a banking system, wherein information is taken from one head and deposited into another. They refer to students as "little vessels, arranged in order, ready to have imperial gallons of facts poured into them until they were full to the brim."[16] Yet they fail to recognize the play (and consequences) of their metaphors. They take their imagery for granted and, as a result, it goes unchallenged and presents itself without limit. The teachers never consider blind spots in their language and approach. Imagination isn't absent from their educational work; rather, their inattention to it congeals into an overwhelming, self-righteous arrogance.

Neglect of imagination doesn't halt its operation, however. Dickens knows that imagination is too natural and powerful a feature of human intelligence to be destroyed outright. Even when belittled and attacked, imagination survives, albeit in stunted forms. It ceases to operate as an active force for understanding the world and devolves, instead, into a means of diversion and escape. No longer recognized as essential to the apprehension of what-is, people seize upon imagination as a tool to avoid it. Imagination becomes sheer entertainment, a side-show, an escape into virtual realities. In the novel, crippled imagination survives in flights of lying and deception, revealing itself via inventive forms of hypochondria, clever advertisements, and the desperate daydreams that enable characters to survive. We must give image to the world we inhabit, shaping and organizing information out of meaningless data. Neglect of the imagination is blindness to the play of images that already shape our lives, thoughts, and relationships. Images, unacknowledged as such, petrify into hardened fact. In the process, we grow inattentive to the possibility of alternatives and to the penumbra of mystery that encompasses everything we know. We sacrifice questioning, wonder, and reverence, all of which demand the imaginative recognition that life is always more than we think it is.

Hard Times concentrates on the lives of certain youngsters as they work their way through Gradgrind's "educational" system. One character, a young girl by the name of Sissy Jupe, comes to the school having been raised in a circus. Her father, succumbing to alcoholism and depression, leaves Sissy with his circus friends, hoping that they can provide the family and education that he cannot. Agreeing to her father's desire that Sissy receive an education, they arrange for her to study in Gradgrind's school.

The fit is painful. Sissy has been raised among kindly, gregarious people. She has grown up in the midst of a rich, chaotic soup of fable, song, and fairytale. She's familiar with animals and colorful personalities. Her circumstances, though challenging in many ways, have insulated her from the rigidity and competitive meanness of Gradgrind's school. She knows close relationships and sympathetic kindness.

Sissy boards in the Gradgrind household and comes to know the headmaster's children Louisa and Tom (and, later, Jane). Raised by their father's insistence on fact, starved of wonder and real relationships, they are chronically bored and desperately unhappy. As the novel unfolds, we watch Tom grow into a relentless manipulator willing to twist his sister's love for him into a means of self-advancement. Louisa survives by slipping into a form of emotional anesthesia. She becomes a doormat, willing to marry the insufferable industrialist Mr. Bounderby at the urging of her brother, largely because she lacks any vision of her own future. Her starved imagination leaves her clueless about the workings of her heart. The consequences of her awful marriage nearly cost her life.

Please forgive the mini-lecture on Dickens' text, but if you haven't read the book, perhaps this brief retelling gives a sketch of his rich and moving novel. In any case, this work would be the focus in the class ahead. My plan for these long evening classes was to assign two students to give short presentations on the reading, thereby offering them a chance to speak in public and have a break from listening to me. The assignment was pretty straightforward: focus on a theme or issue that interests you in the reading, show how the author addresses it, and indicate your agreement or disagreement with what you think the text is saying.

One of the students scheduled to speak on *Hard Times* tonight was a shy woman named Darcy. Until now, she had barely said a word in an otherwise lively class. If I called upon her, she would respond but only briefly, hesitantly, as if mistrusting her own voice. She seemed like someone who would gladly merge into the background of cinderblocks if she could. She was short, wore glasses, and had long hair that fell over her face like a curtain.

For the first time in the semester, on the day of the class, Darcy knocked on my door during office hours. I asked her in, already suspicious about the timing of her visit. She quickly confirmed my misgivings. "I know it's not a great time to bring this up," she whispered, "but I can't do the presentation tonight." She looked down as if studying the carpet. "I've read the assignment, but I'm not making any connections." A long pause ended with, "Maybe I could do a presentation later in the semester on a different book. Sorry if this screws things up a bit."

Listening to Darcy, two personalities grappled in me. One was the academic who had given an assignment and was instead receiving an excuse. His unspoken thoughts streamed out: *Unbelievable. You're letting me know four hours before class that your presentation isn't ready. No prior notice of difficulty or request for help. Is this how you take responsibility for other things in your life? If I let you postpone this presentation, does it simply buttress a bad habit?* Annoyance gave rise to other judgments and questions. *This assignment isn't difficult. How could you not find anything to say about this novel? You're bailing out at a point where you give me no options. Is this intentional? Is it a strategy?*

The other persona was that of a teacher, who processed Darcy's words differently: *Why is she blocked? What's preventing her from making connections? How can she find nothing to say?* The questions coalesced around Darcy's sense of isolation from the text. *What accounts for it? Can anything be done?* The teacher's first impulse was not to judge but to grapple with her learning (or lack thereof); with this inclination came the realization that he barely knew this person.

I stared at Darcy as if facing a cipher. I felt lost. This sudden, painful sense of not knowing her underlines the difference between the academic and the teacher. The academic focuses on a discipline, seeking to gain and impart knowledge, looking to make contributions to a field. The teacher's awareness gravitates toward the person and the question of how learning can occur. The academic gives instruction about a subject; the teacher knows that, first and foremost, he is teaching people.

In this instance, the teacher trumped the academic. Although I remained frustrated to learn about Darcy's difficulty so soon before class, I swallowed the lecture on disappointment. But what to do? I sat for a time without a clue, dimly recognizing that the silent waiting must be uncomfortable for Darcy. Finally, an idea jiggled on the line. I looked up and asked her, "Would you be willing to try an experiment?"

Her face was blank, and, after much delay, she eked out an unenthusiastic, "I guess."

I glanced at my watch. "Let's see, it's three fifteen. You have nearly four hours before class. Go back to the novel and choose one character—anyone you like. Pay close attention to that person, see what she notices, consider how he acts and thinks and feels. Observe the life. Then ask yourself what, if anything, the person's way of being has to do with imagination." I scanned her face for some sign of enthusiasm. All I found was dull resignation that her presentation, like a recurrent nightmare, wasn't going away. I could see her displeasure and her fear at the prospect of taking a public risk, so I threw her one further rope. "I know you're not happy with this idea, so let's make a deal. If the experiment works and you have something to present, then give me a wink when I enter class. No wink and you can present at another time."

After she left, I wondered about the wisdom of the experiment. The academic in me wasn't yielding quietly. *What you've done is to remove all pressure, and that doesn't accomplish anything. Life doesn't come with safety winks.* But the teacher wasn't retreating either. *Yes, Darcy may use the experiment as an easy way out, but why not give her the benefit of the doubt? Why assume that she'll misuse the opportunity?* I was suddenly reminded of a line in *Hard Times*. Sleary, the old circus ringmaster, repeats it several times. In fact, he refers to it as his philosophy: "Make the betht of uth, not the wurtht" ("Make the best of us, not the worst").[17] Though he wouldn't label his motto in this way, it's his appeal for compassion. Unfortunately, the message is lost on the Gradgrind educated.

That evening, I entered class, my eyes peeled for Darcy. She was there at the end of the tables that formed a rectangle. I moved to a seat opposite her, waiting for a sign. She glanced up and (I was pleased to see) winked—not a quick flick of the eyelid but, as I do, by scrunching half her face. After some opening remarks, I suggested starting with a presentation and turned to Darcy. She lowered her head, as she had in my office; bending into the pages before her, she started to read.

"A couple of hours ago, I had nothing for this presentation. Nothing. It bothered me that I couldn't get into the book. Sitting in the library this afternoon, I tried to focus on someone I found interesting. The character I kept returning to was Gradgrind's daughter, Louisa. Several things interested me about her. They're small details, but I find them significant. One is her thing with fireplaces. Sounds strange, I know, but throughout the novel, Louisa is drawn to fireplaces. We often see her staring into them, watching flames subside and embers drop through metal grates. It's a curious habit, and one I share. Why does Dickens call attention to it? What does it say about Louisa? My first guess was that it had to do with Louisa's boredom. Her life is so controlled that she doesn't know what to do with herself.

"There's more to it, though. Why *do* we look into fireplaces? I think it's for the same reason we gaze at clouds. They're invitations to daydream. We stare into them and find images for a lot of things: faces, figures, animals, even ourselves. Louisa may not know it, but I think she finds an image of herself in the embers falling through the fire grate. Her upbringing and education have given her so little fuel, so little air to breathe, that she senses the energies of her life flickering out.

"The other thing that gets me is the scene where Louisa's father tells her that Mr. Bounderby, the wealthy industrialist, is going to ask her to marry him. When she's told this, Louisa asks her father an odd question: 'Do you think I love Mr. Bounderby?'[18] When I first read this, I thought she was being sarcastic, as if to berate her father for not knowing how she felt. But after going over this section again, I came to a different conclusion. Louisa is sincerely asking her father whether she loves Bounderby, because she doesn't know what love is and whether she's feeling it. How could she? She's never been asked about her emotions. Raised without stories of princesses and Cinderellas, without wolves, trolls, and monsters, she doesn't know how to cope with feelings or even recognize what she feels. This is another terrible price of her 'education.' Her knowledge of facts has never given her knowledge of herself.

"When she decides to marry Bounderby, it's really by default. It's a coin-flip out of emptiness. She marries because she has no sense of anything better to do and because her brother has been pushing it. She marries to please him. Since she's never been encouraged to picture her life, she's an empty slate that others write on. Louisa is especially susceptible to the influence of others and is willing to fulfill their wishes, because her own have so little shape."

At this point in Darcy's presentation I was breathing a sigh of relief. I was pleased for her and, given the short time to prepare it, impressed with her analysis. She had paid attention to the details of Louisa's life and had begun to connect them to the imaginative poverty of her schooling. The experiment seemed to be working. She was getting through the talk. I was unprepared, however, for the next statements that she blurted out. She spoke them into the papers before her, but she meant for them to be heard.

"Doing this assignment was frightening for me. It's not that I hate speaking in front of you—which, trust me, I do. And it's not that it was written in a rush, which it was. No, what's frightening is the realization that Louisa is me. I don't like saying this. But it's true, and here's why. Like Louisa, I don't find college all that interesting. I do my work, take my classes, but I have this sense of going through the motions. I do what's necessary, but that's about it. Guess you could say I know what it's like to watch embers flicker out. I don't have much fire in my studies. I see it sometimes in others but not in myself."

Listening to Darcy, I worried whether she was getting too self-confessional. I tried to read the class, but couldn't—other than to note the absolute stillness. I held my peace. Darcy continued.

"I even got pushed into making this presentation tonight. I wanted to get out of it, but our Prof wouldn't let me, or at least not easily. Something clicked, though, when I could see myself in Louisa. It made a difference. In the library this afternoon, I had the sense of reading me.

"I've been studying in Gradgrind's school throughout my life and, like Louisa, I'm doing it because I have to. I suppose it's leading somewhere, but I have little sense of where that somewhere is. I'm stuffed with courses like Louisa is stuffed with facts. I take in information and spit it out when required. I do it for the promise of a decent job. And when I become doubtful that the job is there at the end, my motivation unravels. I keep going, though. Just like Louisa, I do it because I can't find a reason not to. She, I, and maybe you need to gain more knowledge of ourselves, and I can see now that this knowledge requires imagination. *Hard Times* has helped me see this and face it in myself. I don't think my imagination has been destroyed, but I'm going to have to work to reclaim it. That's about it, I guess."

Darcy had hardly looked up from her notes. She could only speak by shutting out her surroundings. Having stopped, she raised her head, as if surfacing from a dive, and glanced around timidly. Clearly, she was finished. A long, awkward silence ensued. Then, to my surprise and for the first and only time in the semester, the class broke into spontaneous applause. They clapped and continued clapping, ramping it up as if to emphasize that it wasn't an act of polite approval or protective backslapping. It was heartfelt thanks.

Darcy's honesty had moved them; they had witnessed, firsthand, the spark of imaginative connection that understands one thing in terms of another. They also had encountered a vivid example of compassionate intelligence. Darcy lit up the dark, painful corners of Louisa's life with embers of her own, and her classmates were acknowledging and celebrating her act of personal imaginative inquiry.

I don't remember much else of the class. That burst of applause was its defining moment. I recall baseball caps shuffling rapidly to the door as class ended, eager to know whether we were, indeed, responsible for the Red Sox winning. I moved more slowly, packing my papers deliberately, waiting for the chance to speak with Darcy. As the room emptied, I caught her eye.

"So, how do you think it went?"

For the first time all evening, a smile blossomed. "I had fun," she said.

"That's important," I replied. "Did you notice how closely the class was listening to you?"

She nodded. "I did."

"How do you feel?" I asked.

"Pretty good," she responded. "I was wicked nervous at first, but I calmed down. I was on safe ground. I know Louisa pretty well." She winked once again with half her face, and both of us laughed. With that, we said our goodnights, and I shut off the lights.

I hoped that the class would be a turning point for Darcy. Unfortunately, that scenario didn't take place. The following week and for the remainder of the semester, she retreated back into her shell, poking her head out only if I called on her. I don't know why. She didn't appear uncomfortable or embarrassed, but it was clear from her lack of interaction with me and her classmates that she preferred to stay within herself. Nevertheless, she finished the course and her writing improved to an extent. Yet her return to silence raised questions. I wondered whether she had really learned something, whether her presentation had signaled the change for which I had hoped. Had it made any difference? As is so often the case in teaching, I didn't really know. The evidence was inconclusive. Apart from her presentation, she disclosed little about herself, and I didn't want to pry. So the silence continued. Others things intruded, time passed. Students went off and new faces replaced them.

Three years after the course, I received an envelope in the mail. Inside was a photograph of Darcy on what looked to be a beach in the Caribbean. A young man sporting cut-off jeans and a broad smile was holding her hand. They looked happy and wonderfully tanned (something we notice here in

Maine). I turned the photo over; scrawled across its back was "The One Thing Needful." The words were vaguely familiar, but I couldn't place them.

I propped the photo on a shelf above my desk. It was good to see Darcy. She looked buoyant, less withdrawn. Her hair was cut attractively, and she was smiling. But the context for the photo and the words was missing. Why had she sent them? What was she saying? My first clue was the realization that the words are the title of *Hard Times'* opening chapter. I hadn't really paid attention to them and (to be honest) hadn't probed what Dickens meant by them. I started to reread the opening chapter of the novel and traced its title back to a message in the Gospel of Luke that points to love as "The One Thing Needful."[19] But why had Darcy sent the photo and message to me now?

My first guess was that she was announcing her engagement or honeymoon. But wouldn't she simply say so? My thoughts kept moving back and forth between the photo and my memory of Darcy's presentation; soon the movement opened up other possibilities. I recalled how, in class, Darcy had related Louisa's obsession with fireplaces and ignorance of her own heart to herself. Was this connection related to the picture and its words?

Suddenly, the haze surrounding the photo started to lift. The picture wasn't an engagement notice or, if it were, it wasn't only that. It was the counter image to Louisa seeing herself in the embers. As corny as it sounds, the picture was of Darcy's flame—not simply in the sense of her boyfriend or fiancé—but in the discovery of her passion. Maybe it was just a teacher's hubris, but I suspected that Darcy was announcing that she finally recognized the connection between imagination and "the one thing needful."

Imagination allows us to enter the depths of another, to go beneath the surface, even to the point of conceiving that other person as part of ourselves. Love in this sense demands imagination. But the connection works in the other direction as well: for imagination to develop, love is necessary. To imagine anything or anyone deeply, to devote time to the unseen and the as-yet-unrealized, we must care.

The answer hit me like a slap: Darcy's photo was the completion of her presentation. It was the resolution to the matter that had bugged me throughout the semester—had the presentation made any difference? Here was my answer. Yes, she had made the connection. The experiment might have taken longer than either of us expected, but it had succeeded. It had borne fruit.

Some will say, of course, that evidence for my conclusion is pretty slim, that it leaps way beyond the facts. If forced to justify my conviction, I'd probably have to admit to guesswork. But in my teacher's heart, I have no doubt. Maybe it's part of the inveterate hope that teaching requires: It aims at what it cannot see. It's predicated on possibility. It's full of fancy, if you like. But hope has its own down-to-earth strength, leading one to search for and perhaps discover evidence that is otherwise easy to overlook. I had witnessed Darcy's isolation in class. I had seen imagination at work when she'd spoken of seeing Louisa in herself. In the photo, I recognized unstudied pleasure in Darcy's face. The contrast between the two was palpable, and their connecting thread was her presentation on Dickens' novel. Yes, I was sure: this picture was Darcy's sign that she had finally realized the connection between love and imagination.

I found myself smiling. As I continued scanning the photo, however, my attention shifted from Darcy to her companion, and I was forced to confront a disturbing fact—sitting atop the young man's head on his slightly tilted cap, gleamed one of life's truly threatening, unsettling symbols, an emblem from the dark side: against a deep blue background, the unmistakable white logo of the New York Yankees. My smile wavered momentarily. A philosophical calm returned, however, as I thought, *Good for you, Darcy; only a loving imagination could overcome so much.*

FOUR

Mildred

"WHY DO IT?" I LOOKED INTO THE MOIST EYES OF the aged lady opposite me. "Why put yourself through it? For what?"

Mildred sat with her hands folded in her lap and, after a minute or so, reached into her pocketbook, pulled out a linen handkerchief, and dabbed her eyes.[20] I felt as downcast as the weather: a somber February day, the sun already descending at 3:30 in the afternoon, my office seeming like an overstuffed closet, and I spending my time reducing an elderly woman to tears. Ever the lady, Mildred refused to blame her red eyes on me.

"Sorry, Professor. It's hard to explain the need to continue. It's a long, complicated story, and, at my age, you do what you have to do. I regret being the bearer of bad news and appreciate your listening. Thanks."

Mildred gathered her purse and leather briefcase and moved to stand. "Oh, before I forget, I do have one piece of *good* news. Remember that creative writing assignment I mentioned a couple of weeks ago, the one I kept revising? Well, I finally got it back from my English professor. She loved it, said that it was the best piece of writing I've done all semester—a straight A."

"That's great. I'd love to read it sometime."

"Really? I'd be honored," she replied and, without missing a beat, dove into her briefcase, surfacing with the paper. "I hope you enjoy it."

"Thanks, Mildred; maybe after I read it, we can get together and talk it over?" For the first time in our acquaintance, I leaned forward and gave her a hug, rather than the standard handshake.

After Mildred left, I slumped in my chair, feeling the gloomy afternoon close in on me. Mildred, the oldest philosophy major I had ever taught, had just told me that she had cancer and would be starting an elaborate battery of chemotherapy and radiation treatments. Afraid that she wouldn't be able to keep up with classes during the regimen, she asked if we could make special arrangements. It was at this point that I had pressed her about why she felt the need to continue her coursework.

"Wouldn't it be better to take some time off and attend to your health? Why pile on the added pressures of classes, readings, and papers? Why not give yourself a break?" Mildred's eyes started to fill up. In retrospect, although I was sorry that my questions had brought her to tears, I was convinced that I was right; she was taking on too much without needing to do so. *For God's sake, Mildred, you're dealing with cancer, not a cold.* My ruminations stalled for the moment, I gulped the last bit of cold coffee and started to close up shop. As I gathered my things, I glanced down at Mildred's paper on top of the desk. I picked it up and began to read.

Before sharing the paper's contents, let me provide a bit more context for her office visit. Mildred was a student in my introductory philosophy course. In a sea of fresh, eighteen to twenty-five year old faces, she stood out, with her coifed silver hair, flower print dresses, and embroidered sweaters. But she was notable for more than her seniority and appearance. Unlike many of her classmates, who had a studied air of nonchalance about college, Mildred was unabashedly eager. She came to class as if she were first violin in a symphony orchestra—meticulously prepared, always seated in the front row, and dressed for the occasion. Her proximity offered me a clear view of her obsessions; for example, she highlighted texts with multiple colored markers and never sat in class without a dictionary under her chair. Although serious about college, she wasn't dour; her work ethic was balanced by a lightness of spirit. She laughed easily, with that no-holds-barred abandon that often graces elderly women. She enthusiastically praised her younger classmates (a demographic that encompassed everyone in the room) and seemed, in short, relentlessly pleased to be in college.

I quickly grew to like Mildred. She reminded me in many ways of my mother—a slight, fragile-looking lady whose small frame concealed a dynamo of energy and determination. Mildred's fascination with her classmates was contagious. She wanted to know what they thought, where they were from, what their plans were. If they had pierced noses and colorful tattoos, she would gravitate to them even faster. From her seat in the front of the room, she would swivel around whenever someone spoke behind her. She enjoyed their company, and they, in turn, appreciated her. They respected her determination and listened when she spoke. But her gratitude for the opportunity to learn made the greatest impression on both them and me. She would often say, right in the midst of some discussion, how grateful she was to be reading Plato or Aristotle, Tolstoy or Thoreau at this point in her life. The same remark, coming from someone else, someone younger, would have seemed fawning, but from Mildred its genuineness was unassailable. The honesty of her gratitude and its unstudied expression punctured the armor of her classmates' nonchalance. It struck me that Mildred, though unaware of it, wielded a surprisingly powerful bobby pin—a simple thankfulness for learning—that jabbed those who regarded the university as a prison from which they sought release.

Mildred simply couldn't hide her delight to be in college. Instead of being obnoxious, though, her delight was endearing and infectious. I enjoyed seeing her classmates' fondness for her, even though she was shameless about relying upon her newfound friends. Frequently, she announced that the one barrier threatening to prevent her from attaining her degree was the infernal math department. She described a life-and-death struggle with some math proficiency course and lobbied for all the tutoring help she could find. Periodically, algebra-assistance payments in the form of chocolate chip cookies made their way around the room before class.

Two events mark my early experience of Mildred. The first was the day she announced her decision to become a philosophy major. She said that she couldn't imagine doing anything more worthwhile with her time than conversing with the philosophers she was reading. She added that, in retirement, she didn't have to worry about putting food on the table or making a career. "I'm over careers," I remember her saying. "At my age, I'm into immediate gratification."

The second event was more disturbing. About a third of the way through the course, I scheduled an in-class essay exam. As usual, I sat reading at a table in the front of the room. Occasionally, I'd look up from my book at flying pens and cramping fingers. As I watched, I noticed that Mildred looked unwell. She held her forehead in one hand and wore an anxious look uncommon for her. I approached her and asked if anything were wrong.

"I don't know, Professor, the old thoughts just aren't there." She smiled weakly, but the fear was plain in her eyes.

I had no idea what was happening. Nearly all the other students had handed in their exams, but Mildred remained in her chair. With time running out, she gave me the exam booklet, saying that she couldn't finish. I looked quickly at the work.

"It's barely half done, Mildred."

"I know," she said. "I can't explain it." She turned and walked to the door. I caught up to her in the hallway.

"Are you sure you're all right?"

A feeble smile barely altered her apprehensive expression. "Well, I felt better before the exam."

"Were you pressed for time? Do you have a history of trouble with in-class exams?"

"No," she replied, "I just couldn't organize my thoughts."

The whole situation didn't seem right to me. Here was a student who was always prepared, who completed the readings and worked hard. But she couldn't finish more than half the exam? *It wasn't* that *difficult*, I thought, and made a split-second decision.

"Listen, Mildred, maybe you're not used to in-class essay exams; maybe time pressure affected you. Why don't you take your exam booklet over to the library and finish it? Bring it back to my office when you're done."

Mildred greeted the proposal with little enthusiasm, taking the exam with the uncharacteristic attitude of *let's just get this thing over with.*

"All right," she said in a low voice, "I'll see what I can do."

As I walked back down the hall, a number of thoughts raced through my mind: *What did I just do, giving Mildred an extension that I hadn't offered to anyone else? How fair is that? I don't know whether other students in the class wrote under time pressure or had similar difficulties completing their exams.* It was a tough call. If one of her classmates were to confront me about favoritism, whether my action violated the notion of equal treatment, I wouldn't have known what to say. I just knew that Mildred wasn't right—which didn't seem much of a justification for bending the rules. *Nice little ethical dilemma*, I thought and pushed it aside.

About two hours later, Mildred knocked on the office door and turned in the exam. We talked for a bit about whether the additional time had made a difference.

"It helped some, I guess. I didn't have to watch the minutes pass. I worried less," she said. "But I'm afraid that I still didn't do well. Everything seemed jumbled."

I tried to cheer her up. "Well, at least it's over. Maybe it isn't as bad as you think."

"Perhaps you're right," she responded dubiously. "I'm just going to go home and take a long nap."

Mildred was right about her performance on the exam; it was in complete contrast to the rest of her work. But we moved on. I felt lucky that none of her classmates had challenged me about the unequal treatment. Maybe no one had noticed. Mildred seemed more subdued in class than before the exam, but I still enjoyed her presence, her good observations and questions. The semester went along.

This is the context for Mildred walking into my office that dim February afternoon. We talked—I forget about what, but I do remember wondering in the midst of our chitchat why she had come. As if reading my thought, she turned suddenly serious: "There's something I have to tell you. Remember when I took that exam, and you let me complete it in the library? "

"Yes, I remember it very clearly," I replied.

"Well, for weeks before then I hadn't been feeling well. I'd been experiencing severe headaches and fatigue. I finally got myself to my doctor and underwent some tests—actually, a lot of them. The results came in a couple of days ago. The report isn't good. I have a brain tumor, and it's malignant." She read my shock and immediately tried to soften the blow: "The tumor must have been stealing space from thoughts on Plato."

Her smile didn't help. The news jolted me, literally. I started fumbling with expressions of sorrow, even foolishly asking how serious the cancer was.

"It's serious," she said, with dreadful simplicity.

I groped my way to the usual questions: Was there anything I could do? Did she have family in the area? She answered that she had good friends in her apartment complex, and nieces and nephews lived nearby. Her main concern was to tell me that she didn't know whether she'd be able to attend classes and, if not, to ask if she could complete the course some other way.

I was amazed that she was even thinking about finishing the semester. The work seemed so insignificant in relation to what she was facing. I pushed my questions about why, at her age and in this situation, she felt this need. Mildred was not, however, inclined to heed my advice that she withdraw. Recognizing her resistance, I relented.

"Don't worry; we'll find a way for you to finish. If you can't come to class, we'll complete the course online or meet at your apartment—especially if chocolate chip cookies are in the offing," I ended, hoping to provide a bit of comic relief.

She seemed genuinely relieved. "I appreciate that, Professor. I've got my heart set on finishing." It was then that she moved to rise, told me of her English paper, and handed it to me.

I don't know why, but I couldn't leave the office without reading it. I wanted to get out, but the news of Mildred's cancer exerted a strong contrary pull to stay with her words. I began reading begrudgingly, but, as usual with Mildred, her charm and directness undid my resistance.

Her paper "An Incredible Woman" is about her mother, Albertina. It opens on a snowy Sunday afternoon with Mildred listening to the chime of her grandmother's clock in the hallway. The peaceful stillness of Mildred's apartment turns her thoughts to memories of the past, and she takes down a box filled with photographs of family and friends from the top shelf of the hall closet. The first photo that draws her attention is of Albertina's graduation from St. Patrick's grammar school in 1919. Of this occasion, Mildred writes:

All thirty students with somber faces are standing rigid in their high-buttoned shoes in front of the brick school building. The boys are dressed in knickers and jackets that look too small on them, and the girls in their prim and proper high collared blouses with long skirts. In the second row, third on the right, with sparkling eyes and a slight smile, is Albertina, my mother.

She was the oldest in a family of six children, two girls and four brothers. Albertina's mother and father were immigrants from Lithuania. Her father came from a wealthy family and was well educated. Her mother grew up as a peasant on a small farm. They met, fell in love, and decided to journey to the New World. Albertina's father sold his land inheritance to his brother to finance their voyage. They left everything behind and came to America, settling in a small mill town in New England.

Mildred then focuses particularly on her mother's upbringing and education:

During the early nineteen hundreds, men and women's roles were rigidly defined. Grammar school education, which was up through eighth grade, was considered sufficient for the young women of the working class. After graduation from grammar school, if a girl made it that far, she went to work in the mill or got married…

Albertina, upon graduation, expressed her deep desire to go to high school. This announcement brought forth her mother's beliefs in a very firm proclamation: "Education is wasted on women! A woman's place is in the home! To raise a family!"[21]

Albertina was devastated. She couldn't understand why her brothers had a choice but she didn't. She couldn't understand why education would be wasted on a woman. She couldn't understand why a woman's place was only in the home, raising a family. Many times, when she found her mother alone in the kitchen, she pleaded, "Why, Mama? Tell me why."

Albertina was very close to her father. They used to spend hours together reading and talking. Her father recognized the brilliance of her mind and believed in his daughter's dream of an education. At her urging, he promised to re-raise the possibility of high school with her mother.

The task of changing his wife's mind proved very difficult. Mildred describes Albertina lying in bed, anxiously listening to muffled voices in another room and knowing the cause of the heated discussion. After a week of struggle, her mother agreed that Albertina could go to high school, but only on the condition that she would also work part-time in the mill. The young woman accepted the terms with jubilation.

Mildred details the labor that made her mother's schooling possible: She worked in the mill Monday through Friday from 3:00 to 8:00 in the evening, in addition to completing a considerable list of chores at home. She would rise once a week at 4:00 a.m. to scrub the laundry and, on two other days, wash the kitchen floor before running off to school. Mildred's commentary deserves attention:

> Sunday afternoon, the dishes cleared away, was a time of relaxing or visiting with guests. Sometimes Albertina studied in the afternoon and into the evening so as to make it easier for herself during the week. There were times when she found the going tough, especially during her menstrual period when she was more tired and energy drained. Those were the times Albertina cried into her pillow at night, whispering prayers to give her courage and strength to reach her goal. Never a murmur or a word of discouragement was uttered by Albertina to her family, especially her mother,

about how hard it was at times keeping up with everything and going to high school.[22]

Mildred also writes of her mother's dedication to her studies and how she found power and enjoyment in the classroom. In 1923, upon graduation from high school, Albertina was awarded a scholarship to Bates College due to outstanding grades in Latin; however, success brought renewed trouble.

Albertina's announcement of the scholarship and her wish to accept it rekindled her mother's disdain for education, and she used the scholarship itself against her daughter: "You don't need Latin to run your home or raise your children, at least I didn't. I'm sure millions of other women around the world are doing fine without Latin." Once again, Albertina sought the help of her father. Mildred captures the ensuing struggle:

It was a reenactment of the 1919 event, with a different conclusion. Far into the night, the whole household again was disturbed with the muffled voices that carried argumentative tones. Joseph in his heartfelt battle tried to make Anna realize that their daughter had special talents and it would be a shame to have them go to waste. But, this time, he lost the fight for Albertina in Anna's court of law. Her last word was a resounding "No" to the college education issue.

Thereafter, the nights were quiet except for the sound of soft weeping that could be heard now and then coming from Albertina's room. She wondered what her life was going to be like now. She loved the academic world and was going to miss it terribly.[23]

Albertina's life was forever changed by her mother's decision. In 1923, she met Anthony, a neighbor's nephew who was visiting from a nearby town. He was six feet tall, dark haired, and very handsome and charming. He worked as a laborer in a paper mill and freelanced as an amateur wrestler, challenging travelling wrestlers at state fairs for purse money. Anthony was known as "Bangor Bill" in the wrestling circuits ("Bangor Tony" just didn't sound right). Anthony's visits to his aunt became quite frequent after he met Albertina. But, as with her college scholarship, their relationship was destined to meet with disapproval and resistance, particularly from her mother. Any man who went carousing around state fairs and fighting for money wasn't right for her daughter.

But Bangor Bill fell in love with Mildred's mother and, despite obstacles, asked her to marry him. As Albertina later told her younger sister, she liked Anthony but didn't believe that she loved him. Anthony persisted, however, and she eventually agreed to become his bride. Her decision only heightened her mother's reservations, but Albertina ignored her mother's warnings and made her wedding plans. Mildred describes her mother's wedding day:

> The day arrived. Albertina was in her bedroom getting dressed for the wedding. Her mother entered as the veil was being placed on Albertina by her sister. Albertina was an angelic vision in her high-collared white gown with lace over satin that fitted tightly at the waist and fell into soft folds throughout the skirt. Albertina turned and faced her mother. They stood for a moment in silence. The sunlight was shining through her window on her lovely auburn-colored hair that framed her face under the veil. There was a misty aura about the beautiful bride-to-be.
>
> Mother and daughter stared at each other. Anna broke the quiet and said with a quiver in her voice, "Please, Alber-

tina, it's not too late to change your mind. Anthony is going to give you a hard life. I just know it. Please reconsider. Don't marry him."

Albertina, for the first time in her life, stood up to her mother. She crossed the room to face her. "Let me go to Bates College, and I'll remove my veil."

Anna's face grew grim as she replied weakly, "Albertina, I'd rather see you get married to Anthony than waste your life going to school."

With tears in her eyes, Albertina turned to her sister and said, "It's time to go." She moved out of the sunlight, past her mother, and into the arms of her father, who was waiting at the bedroom door.

Anthony and Albertina were married that morning at St. Patrick's church.[24]

Mildred's mother never earned a degree. Later in life, after her marriage had failed, she found a position in a university library, which kept her close in some ways to a world of books, ideas, and Latin. The essay ends with Mildred speaking of the hatbox she had taken down:

> With a heavy heart, I return the grammar school photo to the box, wondering what might have been if my mother's dream had come true. A few glimpses flash through my imagination: Albertina in her cap and gown, ascending the stage to receive her degree at the Bates College graduation ceremonies, then going on for her Master's and Doctorate in the field of Latin Studies.
>
> As I place the cover on the hatbox, I'm thinking that there is a spark of ambition in each of us to accomplish dreams, which can be fanned into flame by encouragement, or just

remain a flicker in oneself where dreams are never brought to light.

The rose tapestry-covered box filled with memories of extraordinary people is back on the shelf for another time.[25]

Almost instinctively, I raised a hand to cover my mouth and held my breath, knowing that I had witnessed something powerful, deep, and good. Even the dismal afternoon, now turned to evening, couldn't dispel the sense of wonder and clarity engendered by the story. I now understood Mildred's refusal to drop her courses. It was an act of familial love. Mildred was fighting for the degree denied to her mother so many years before.

Over the next month or so, Mildred found it increasingly difficult to attend class, so we decided to meet occasionally in her apartment to discuss the readings. Our get-togethers, however, were more about tea, cookies, and free-ranging conversation than Aristotle's *Ethics*. She was too weak. Eventually, she proposed taking an incomplete grade for the course and completing it the following semester. Instead of visits, we would speak on the phone every few weeks. But with end-of-semester busyness, the arrival of summer, and my travel overseas, our contact became less frequent.

That fall, I received a call from a retired colleague with whom I hadn't spoken in years. He said that Mildred was a member of his church and had mentioned that I was one of her professors.

"I haven't spoken with her in nearly a month. How's she doing?" I asked.

"She's dying" was his blunt reply. "The reason I'm calling," he continued, "is that I'd like your help in trying to get the university to grant her a bachelor's degree. She doesn't have the required number of credits, but she isn't going to make it. Something has to be done, and now. Are you willing to help?"

"I'll do anything I can," I promised.

Our first step was a letter of appeal to the president of the university explaining the situation. We waited. And waited. Frustrated with the lack of action, we agreed to pester his office tag-team style with requests for information. A resultant letter from the president informed us that our request was extremely delicate and required careful consultation with the chancellor and board of trustees. Awarding an honorary bachelor's degree without the specified number of credits was a complicated matter. It could not be done haphazardly, and time was needed to do it right.

The irony, of course, was that time was the one asset that Mildred lacked. My colleague and I decided that, in order to move the process along (and increase pressure), we would invite Mildred to a gathering at the university for her family and friends. She was all for it. We asked her to compile a short list of people whom she'd like to invite. In less than three days, Mildred mailed back a list with one hundred and seventy-six names. I gulped at the sight of it; who was going to pay for a luncheon of this size? My partner in crime told me not to worry, assuring me that as soon as people knew that the event was for Mildred, money would not be an object. To his credit, he was completely right. Respondents to "Mildred's University Party" (we couldn't call it a degree ceremony, as we didn't yet know whether the university's bureaucratic wheels would churn fast enough) were extremely generous.

Shortly before the party was to occur, we received official notice that, yes, the university would award Mildred an honorary bachelor's degree at the luncheon. I reread the letter of announcement several times, realizing, as others could not, that Mildred would be the first woman in her family to obtain a college degree.

To be honest, sitting several tables away, I have no idea of her conversations at the luncheon. I know that she looked immensely happy. When that bachelor's hood was placed over her head and draped across her shoulders, she beamed from head to toe. Of course, she was very weak, so she gave no speech. Just attending the event, dressed to the hilt, was statement enough. For the most part, she sat at the head table, surrounded by nieces and nephews, and looked fulfilled. I remember her individually thanking each of her professors, even the instructor of the dreaded math proficiency course.

At the end of the ceremony, a line of well-wishers formed to congratulate her. As I moved forward, I was recalling the end of the paper she had written about her mother. Earlier, I quoted the first line of the final paragraph. Here it is in full:

> The rose tapestry-covered box filled with memories of extraordinary people is back on the shelf for another time. Another time when another photo of a graduation will be added to the box of memories: Albertina's daughter in a cap and gown with a degree from the university. Her gray hair is tucked under the cap, and under the gown she feels her mother's locket, close to her heart. Mother and daughter are entwined. The mother's spark from long ago, combined with the spark of her daughter, is being mysteriously fanned into flame, a flame bringing forth light to honor Albertina's dream.[26]

Her words have the unashamed affection and sentimental sweetness that often characterize the elderly. One would be mistaken, however, to take them as instances of gauze-like puffery. Mildred pursued her dream with guts and tenacity. She had, after all, a bit of the boxer within her. Her determination to obtain that degree in those, the last days of her life, was breathtaking and inspiring. She was one tough cookie.

I knew as I approached Mildred that I'd best keep my words short. I didn't want to end a lovely ceremony in a puddle of tears. I hugged her thin body, and we exchanged quick kisses on the cheek. She grabbed my hand in both of hers and said that she was very grateful. I put my hands on her shoulders, looked into her eyes, and said, "Congratulations, Mildred. You've made your mom very proud."

FIVE

Among Small
Beauties

AN EVENT TOOK PLACE EIGHTEEN YEARS AGO IN THE basement of a university building. It occurred in silence, without witnesses, executed by a person whom you'll never meet. Despite its obscurity, it's an occurrence that deserves notice and consideration. Just as we characterize certain remarks as pregnant, some deeds warrant the term as well. These acts conspicuously embody the message that they want to impart. Think of the irrepressible leap of an athlete encapsulating the experience of exultant victory, or the gathering hug between old friends capturing the awareness of two people being inseparably and thankfully part of each other's life. The event in that basement was the pregnant act of a teacher.

And not just any teacher. I've been surrounded by teachers my entire life. My mom was a grammar school teacher. I became a college teacher, as did my sister (also of philosophy), and my wife and brother-in-law also teach. In terms of occupations, the family has a severe case of constipated imagination. Throughout my life, I've known more than my fair share of fine educators. But the best teacher I ever met was the person in that basement. His name was Tom Downey.

Evoking Tom's act stems from my abiding interest in the question of what qualities make a good, in this case, an exceptional, teacher. What characteristics distinguish people who teach with genuine grace? How to account for them? Of course, countless educational studies discuss the factors and techniques of good teaching, but we miss something essential if we lose sight of the individuals who give these attributes life. I return to this event for another reason as well, one intensified by the passing years: certain people ought not to be forgotten.

In coming to know someone, it's important not to overlook the obvious, starting with the body (Tom would have pointed out with a wink and grin that philosophers have special need for reminding on this score). My favorite picture of Tom shows him sitting on the steps of a porch with his wife Colleen. His ever-present coffee mug is garrisoned near his right foot. His left hand lightly brushes his wife's leg, while the other doffs a hat (not exactly a cowboy's, but close). His long, reddish brown hair, which he often pulled tight behind his head in a ponytail, is falling over his shoulders. His wiry body is perched, as was his habit, with legs tucked beneath him, as if coiled, ready to spring. Except for a missing guitar, he looks like a musician out of the sixties, a characterization that would not have disappointed him.

But it's his face that dominates the photograph. It's turned upward, as if he were suddenly surprised at something in the sky. His mouth is open, caught (or so it seems to me) in a momentary "ah." The look on his face is hard to summarize, combining as it does an impish sense of delight, the sparkle of laughter, an inclination to wonder. Something else also present is harder to pin down to a feature but is implied in the workman's jacket, jeans, and hat. The body is weather-beaten. The picture shows a person of remarkable lightness, but a lightness earned by one who journeyed long and hard to find it.

In this glimpse of Tom's physical appearance, a basic trait of his personality is evident: his embodiment of disparities. He had, for example, the bent of a gifted scholar committed to poring over ancient texts, who counted among his philosophical friends Plato and Nietzsche, Sophocles and Job. Yet these thinkers joined in Tom the company of Bruce Springsteen and Bob Dylan, Joni Mitchell and Harry Potter. He was an academic but never concealed his love of television sitcoms like *The Simpsons* and his concern for the fate of the Celtics. A passion for coffee and cigarettes was "balanced" by a lifelong commitment to vegetarianism. He had prodigious patience for long, leisurely conversations and an uncanny ability to follow their threads. Yet he was an exceptionally private person, someone who prized solitude as necessary and welcome. The inconsistencies abound.

He seemed to me a walking contradiction. But instead of lamenting or concealing this way of being, Tom embraced it. More accurately, he found humor and strength, even understanding, in his disparities. He was careful not to disown parts of himself to fit some mold—and certainly not to please those in positions of authority. His acknowledgement of these contradictory aspects is part of the reason why so many and

different kinds of people were attracted to Tom. He was unashamed of both his normality and his uniqueness.
This is not to say that he didn't recognize or wouldn't
change problems within himself. Quite the contrary, he was
very much a restless spirit. Part of his appreciation of solitude stemmed from the quiet necessary to detect the need for
change and the means to effect it. He would often disappear
from friends, sometimes for long periods, and emerge radiating a sense of new paths cleared and charted. The changes,
however, were not imposed from outside or the result of alter-
ing parts of himself that others found troubling or inconve-
nient. Tom had a lifelong "problem with authority," which
is to say, he was an independent spirit, and, although people
praise independence in general and in the abstract, they often
call the person who embodies it a "loose cannon," "maverick,"
or (my personal favorite) "team challenged."

When I met Tom, he was an undergraduate philosophy
major. After graduation, he remained at the university for a
year to help design and launch a fledgling honors program
and then went off to graduate school at Temple University.
Several years after he left, I became director of that program.
Like many educational experiments, Honors was underfund-
ed from the outset. Enthusiasm and commitment made up for
a great deal, but sustained poverty eventually took its toll. At
one point, desperate because of a staffing shortage (when two
faculty members announced the receipt of fellowships abroad
for the same year), I called Tom to ask whether he would have
an interest in teaching with us. He leapt at the offer.

His return gave me a chance to observe how fine a teacher
he had become. Tom was acutely aware that he was teaching
people, not disciplines or subjects. More precisely, he taught
to their intersection. But the riveting feature about Tom and,

I suspect, good teachers in general is not the groundbreaking character of their insights but how fully they live those perceptions. Although it's a platitude to say that teaching occurs in the service of students, the living of this platitude marks a good teacher. Tom knew the names of his students, no matter how large the class. He became acquainted with many of them as individuals: their towns and family backgrounds, sports and instruments, difficulties and plans. His student recommendations were famous for their detail; a colleague once described them as miniature portraits. The vividness of his knowledge about them stemmed from the fact that his students were his unequivocal priority. Never once did I hear him complain that he was too busy to meet with his students. For them, he seemed to have all the time in the world.

Time was, in fact, a major issue that played into his construction and teaching of courses. Like many educators, he knew the pitfalls of "covering material," but, unlike most, he strove relentlessly against it. He was convinced that it was better to work closely with less material than to reach broadly and end up skimming texts. His penchant was to move slowly, with deliberateness evident in the pace of his courses. He refused to rush from one reading or assignment to the next, believing that students need time to encounter the works that they're studying and, inseparably, time to notice and unpack their responses and assumptions. Educators cannot (or at least *should* not) ask students to rush while simultaneously giving them the message that the material is important. Not surprisingly, one of Tom's favorite books was the novel *Momo* by Michael Ende, a story about the destructiveness of "time saving" and the fearsome busyness to which it gives rise.[27]

Implicit in his emphasis on slowing down was a concentration on listening. As I mentioned earlier, he had a remarkable ability to gather the threads of conversations. In classrooms, he could connect and juxtapose the comments of students, collectively and individually. In the presence of such "big ears," they could discover their disagreements with each other and with themselves. This attentiveness underscored, as nothing else, the fact that they mattered. This gift of listening was so pronounced in Tom that one sensed in him the ability to listen *into* people, going beyond what they said to what they did not—the gaps, silences, hesitations, resistances, and deflections.

Tom was also aware that classrooms are often places of pain for people—sites where they had experienced shame and fear, indifference, even cruelty. He was bothered by the terrible irony that education, which presents itself as a means of growth, even liberation, is a setting of punishment for so many. He prized discipline in the form of devoted hard work, but discipline in the sense of inflicting pain and justifying it as motivation, he rejected fiercely. Instead of the stick and carrot, Tom taught by tapping people's thirst for meaning and connection. As someone strongly influenced by Buddhism, he was keenly aware of the extensive, unnecessary suffering that we impose on others and ourselves and tried to diminish it. He acted on his view that classrooms must become spaces in which students might experience delight.

Another of Tom's traits was a deep appreciation of quirkiness—the oddities and idiosyncrasies of people, their telltale habits and characteristic gestures. This gift contributed to the humor in his classes but also went beyond it. When people sense that they can be themselves and are welcomed nonjudgmentally, the diversity of classrooms (a feature that makes them meaningful as places) opens up. People cease to fear that they'll pay a price for honesty; they start speaking their minds. Quirks are more than endearing characteristics; they are portals into lives, especially into traits that have resisted pressures to conform. When smiled upon, they provide a means of lightheartedness and insight. Like the sparkle in eyes, energetic classrooms have a characteristic glint that comes to light as people realize that they are valued just as they are, quirkiness and all.

Of course, the danger in listing these strengths is promoting an illusion that Tom didn't experience educational mishaps and classes gone badly awry. Of course he did; in fact, his care for teaching made him more acutely aware of problems and shortcomings. But even in the midst of such disappointments, he maintained an unwavering belief that teaching is a noble act, an undertaking that matters greatly. To Tom, teaching was not a fallback, default position or a staging area for assaults on the climb to become a famous professor. He inclined more toward basements; the "trenches"; places near the ground, where there is direct contact with the fecund soil that produces and maintains life.

Tom's one characteristic as a teacher that is hardest to explain is also the most central, and the one that I resisted most. Tom talked openly about a spirituality of education, that education's central task is the nourishing of *soul* and *spirit*. I found this language uncomfortable, even dangerous. It smacked of group hugs, gurus, and the prospect of classrooms swaying to the strains of Kumbaya. The terms soul and spirit seemed vague, ill-defined, and the attempt to educate in terms of them opened the door, I thought, to indoctrination and hierarchical control. Institutions of learning, particularly public ones, see the danger of faith substituting for thought and rightly observe the separation of church and state.

No decisive conversation or event changed my thinking; rather, I experienced a gradual ebbing of resistance. Slowly, I came to see that my objections weren't as strong as I thought. The fact that we can't adequately define soul and spirit isn't convincing grounds for their dismissal. As Tom once put it to me: "If we rule out discussion of everything we can't clearly define, conversations would be remarkably short and awfully boring. All that truly matters in life—love, awareness, the taste of chocolate—resist clear definition. We speak of them, nonetheless, and find it important to do so."

My second objection also bit the dust, as I began to realize that it's possible to use the vocabulary of soul and spirit without reference to any religious doctrine. Shortly thereafter, my argument against thought control turned on me as well. In refusing to consider these subjects seriously in education, we make the mistake of ceding to organized religions a monopoly over spirituality, leaving issues related to spirit and soul in the hands of a few, reserving them in many cases for those who are immensely confident of their answers. The consequences of leaving spirituality to the purview of religion are all too evident in the world we inhabit.

Part of my reluctance to think of education in these terms was that I associated spirituality with people who possess, or think they possess, answers—the province of those who have vanquished doubt and confusion. I was mistaken. People strive for greater awareness and appreciation of life from the profound realization that they are without them. Doubt, confusion, ignorance, and pain help to initiate and sustain the spiritual quest. The search to live more fully begins, as it did for Dante and many others, when one is lost in a deep, dark wood and undertakes passage out.[28]

I came to see that, independent of any particular religious tradition, we experience that which the words *soul* and *spirit* try to name. We notice the difference between mechanical actions and those that arise from enthusiasm and care. We sense when people speak from the depths of their beliefs or the "tops of their heads." Soul is the font of who we are, what animates and gives us life. It's the creative energy of being that distinguishes living creatures from corpses. It is, provided one listens and responds to it, the impulse that directs a life.

The airy imprecision that I associated with spirit was correct but for the wrong reasons. I argued that spirit refers to nothing concrete, but I came to recognize that no-thingness pervades our entire experience; indeed, without it, the world of definite things would be impossible. Anything that presents itself to us—a tree, a book, the face of a friend—appears within an invisible matrix of intentions, emotions, memories, ideas, and meaning. This web of relation filters everything we experience. Things emerge from a vast and vital universe, like waves arising from a surrounding sea, and this incredible interdependence is, for the most part, unseen. Our world is filled, paradoxically, with emptiness. Although our attention ordinarily focuses on the particulars before our eyes, these visible entities are possible only on the basis of the overwhelming unseen.

If soul is the source of creative energy, the wellspring of growth and development, spirit is the conscious awareness of it. Spirit is the spreading awareness of soul, as we seek to acknowledge and align ourselves with it. It's present as a craftsperson embodies her awareness and care for wood in the making of a table. It's manifest in the bond of friendship and the relation between parent and child. It's the energy that fuels the enthusiastic teacher. Any action imbued with loving attention recognizes and manifests spirit. It's what connects the depth of one being with that of another. Tom and I talked over these matters at length. But it wasn't just these conversations that helped to break my resistance. What mattered even more was the fact that, as these concepts acquired life, the presence of spirit in teaching became conspicuous. Examples weren't altogether unfamiliar (long ago, I saw that look in my mom's eyes when she talked about her students), but now I had the rudiments of a language to identify what captured my attention. I was witnessing acts that I had trouble passing off as something else. My cynicism was shrinking. I was drawing nearer to understanding the impetus for the event in the basement.

One of Tom's responsibilities in the Honors Program was to teach a section of a course on the European Middle Ages that had been historically troublesome. I don't know why the course lacked student interest. Perhaps it was the strangeness of studying a culture so thoroughly dominated by religion. Perhaps the lives of saints and theologians easily seemed like museum relics to modern sensibilities. Whatever the cause, Tom taught to this presumption of difference. Instead of assuming that we know the concerns that drive the hermit, the mendicant, the espouser of poverty, the god-obsessed, Tom didn't. Instead of approaching medieval figures as quaint, dismissible curiosities, he let them challenge modern suppositions. However he did it, Tom managed to turn the course around. Students began to speak excitedly of Saint Augustine, the Grail legends, Dante, and Saint Francis.

But as the saying goes, "no good deed goes unpunished."[29] Tom's section of the course began to significantly outdraw the other, taught by a member of the English Department and the university's preeminent medievalist. Had I taken the time to put myself in her shoes, I would have realized the sting of having a newcomer, someone without her scholarly record and Ph.D., attract more students. But I didn't; I was just pleased that a troublesome course seemed to be righting itself.

Before long, however, I was fielding questions from students in the program regarding whether Tom's popularity resulted from soft standards. I knew that this wasn't the case. I also knew that such questions are not typically on the list of undergraduate concerns. Questions persisted, however, and I began to trace them to a source. The trail led, like some bad game of academic Clue, to the medievalist in the English Department. The provost of the university (to whom I reported) also started to voice nearly identical concerns and, when pressed for their source, told me that the medievalist had spoken to him for "the good of the program."

I hit the roof. To make such accusations to students and administrators, to make them in private, without disclosure (and, hence, the chance of rebuttal) seemed to me beyond a case of disparagement. I said as much to the medievalist and told her that it had to stop. It didn't. Students continued to be plied with the opinion that someone without a Ph.D. was professionally incompetent to teach an Honors course. With a sick heart, I watched our educational community rupture and shred.

I decided that I couldn't tolerate, and the program couldn't withstand, such disregard of collegial fairness and asked the English professor for her resignation, which she had earlier threatened to tender if Tom remained teaching in the program. The move was politically inept; I acted from frustration and anger and consulted no one. All hell broke loose. Articles, apparently well-orchestrated, were printed in the campus newspaper about a full professor being "fired" (omitting that she would return to her regular schedule of courses in the English Department). Insinuations of sexism surfaced in a letter signed by members of the Women's Studies Program (none of whom bothered to confirm the accusation). University administrators, suddenly confronted with a problem they didn't want, decided that a "review" of the program would be useful. Instead of tackling the issue themselves, however, they executed a safe hand-off of the problem to a faculty committee. The so-called review dragged on for the better part of a year, exhausted everyone, and decided little.

Even now, from a distance of years, returning to those events is painful. What *has* altered is the embattled self-righteousness that I felt at the time. I've concluded that there was ample blindness on everyone's part. I failed to foresee a problem with the uneven popularity of the course's two sections and acted impulsively in demanding the resignation. The medievalist let wounded pride justify repeated acts of disparaging behavior, and university administrators simply played it safe. Tom withdrew into his classes, finding the behavior of colleagues to one another a denial of nearly everything that higher education supposedly stands for. Looking back, there seems to be very little unique about the affair—just another skirmish in the crowded battlefield of academic politics. But it is against and because of this landscape that the event in the basement occurred.

Shortly after the debacle, I sought and obtained a sabbatical. I couldn't wait to get away. A new director was hired from another university. Tom remained, having one year left on his contract. He later told me that the new director, his first day on the job, called Tom into his office and told him that he would not be rehired and should start looking for other employment as soon as possible. No words of regret or appreciation. He wasn't harsh or mean, just impersonal, businesslike. I doubt whether Tom was itching to stay at this point. He'd had enough of university politics and had begun to doubt whether the kind of education he valued was possible in large-scale institutions. He would finish out the year and be off. I think he underestimated, however, the corrosive effects of grinding neglect and how it would feel to operate like a ghost in a place you had helped to create. Hatred is difficult to withstand; indifference is worse.

Tom and I retreated to late-night phone conversations and occasional lunches at remote restaurants. He felt tremendously alone at the university, avoiding the cafeteria and even giving up his usual walks across campus. He found himself uninvited to meetings. His one solace, he said, was being able to close the door of the classroom and, for a time, shut out the rest. He was proud that, until the very end, his students didn't know that he would be leaving. He wanted the courses he taught that year to be among his best. I suspect they were.

Tom's last days in the program were at the end of May. I've often imagined what they were like: the accumulating momentum of hurt as he went through the process of packing his books, cleaning out his desk, closing his office, and negotiating awkward good-byes with colleagues and staff. I don't know whether he was bothered by the fact that the university in general offered not a single note of thanks; he probably didn't expect it. His formal teaching career was over. My sense was that he was overwhelmingly tired and disappointed with how we educators treat each other.

With the spring semester and my sabbatical at an end, I showed up at the program early on a Monday morning to copy some papers. The place was nearly deserted. After finishing my work, I decided to leave from the basement, as I had parked my car in the adjoining driveway. Part of the basement served as a student lounge, with a few stuffed chairs, several desks, a coke machine, some posters, and a blackboard. As I was making my way to the back door, some writing on the blackboard caught my eye. I knew it immediately as Tom's. He must have entered the building over the weekend to finish packing and had come to the basement before leaving. In block letters, he had left this message:

> Students,
>   Work hard, but remember in your studies to laugh and enjoy the small beauties. This is about the heart, the turning of souls; it is a lifetime endeavor, taken one step at a time.

By the time I arrived, some student must have already seen it, for slightly above and to the left of Tom's words was an equally eloquent statement in another hand: "DO NOT RE-MOVE," followed by a string of exclamation marks.

The message hit me like a punch. What stunned me at the time was the sheer fact *that* he had written it. Here was someone who was being unceremoniously shown the door by the university, who never deserved the treatment he received, who was leaving a program he had helped establish, and his thought before going was to write a note to students. I stood there, tears rolling down my cheeks, and copied the words.

The message wasn't carefully planned or crafted; he wrote it on the fly, or so I pictured. The words came out unpolished, quick—without hesitation, which for me enhanced their worth. There was no mistaking from whence they came. They arose from the gut, with a timeless layover in the heart.

They needed no fine-tuning; these words had been at the core of his teaching for many years—they were an extension of a teacher's care for his students. But left as they were, in the obscurity of that basement, they embodied in a single, pregnant gesture the being of a teacher: love, pure and simple.

Since that day, I've had time to consider the message—my way of respecting the "do not remove" request. Some of its statements don't surprise me. The advice about taking one step at a time and remembering to laugh was vintage Tom, as was the thought about education being a matter of the turning of the soul. The message was from someone who knew his Plato well. It was Tom's way of reminding students that the purpose of college isn't to learn how to make a living, it's to learn how to make a life. Why, though, the emphasis on enjoying the small beauties?

Tom knew that the need for beauty is powerful. On a very basic level, we hunger for it, as if beauty supplies a kind of nutrition that is difficult to live without. We respond strongly to its presence. In the midst of beauty we awaken; our senses come alive; our emotions, imagination, and thought are called into play. Perhaps the clearest sign of experiencing beauty is a felt change of consciousness. We become attentive to the world that surrounds us, seeing it as if for the first time. Inherent in this transformation is a realization of the enormity of things: they're richer, fatter, more complex and vibrant than we had realized.

But why stress "*small* beauties?" I take this emphasis as encouragement to seek beauty not only in the recognized places—famous works of art by established artists, important museums—but in unauthorized, uncelebrated, ordinary circumstances. The message, as I interpret it, is the need to uncover beauty in the everyday, to find it in basements and perhaps even classrooms. The words fit the act and vice versa. Still, there was something more. Why leave *these words* as a final statement?

Tom was a spiritual mutt, and one tradition upon which he drew was that of the Shakers. The old Shaker song *Simple Gifts* has given me some insight into an answer to my question:

'Tis the gift to be simple, 'tis the gift to be free
'Tis the gift to come down where we ought to be,
And when we find ourselves in the place just right,
'Twill be in the valley of love and delight.
When true simplicity is gain'd,
To bow and to bend we shan't be asham'd,
To turn, turn will be our delight,
Till by turning, turning we come 'round right.[30]

If I understand the song, the gift is learning to live in the world aright. This learning is truly *the* great gift because, if ever received, the world shows itself—henceforth and no matter the circumstances—as a place of love and delight. The overpowering richness of what-is, down to its smallest and most everyday detail, breaks in upon us. When we recognize the ordinary things and events of our lives as beautiful, love has become a way of being. Awareness of the small beauties is the sign of coming "round right." Beauty happens when we approach life, in all its guises, with attentive love.

Words on a chalkboard can easily seem insignificant and be quickly wiped away by the stroke of an eraser. But grasped as a manifestation of a teacher's love for his students and the act of teaching itself, the dust on the board grows large, fat, and luminous. The same is true with anything, and this idea was the essence of what Tom sought to teach. Taken at surface value, sensed quickly in only their externals, people and objects contract—they become small, barely worthy of notice. But approached lovingly, they expand, spread out in connection, and acquire weight. They show themselves as worthy of attention, even to the point of radiance.

After leaving the university, Tom found a job as a copy editor for legislative bills in the Maine State House in Augusta. It was a dead-end position in terms of career and didn't prefigure any return to the classroom (which had remained my hope for him). Yet he seemed happy, continued to write, and spoke of his fellow workers with affection. Several years after his departure through the basement, he discovered that he had lung cancer. One of the emails I received from him spoke about it:

> Ever since I was a teen, I have speculated on what would happen if I were told that I had a terminal illness. I figured that if I should hear that late in life, I no doubt wouldn't be done dorking around and then would feel that I had to meditate like hell to make up for all the lost time. As it turned out, when I first found out I had cancer, I thought nothing of the sort. Two things hit me immediately and deeply. First I saw how beautiful the world is: the colors and textures, the sounds, the feel of the wind, the animals, the greenery and was overcome with gratitude. Second, I saw how much people need love and how we are called here to love. Petty issues and disgruntlements I had been carrying about people simply vanished through no will of my own. We are here to generate and receive beauty and love. Now I know this is not much as far as insight goes, we have all heard it, but it wasn't so much the message as it was the level

at which it was felt. Due to these gifts, I cannot at all feel victimized by my illness or see it as an enemy to be beaten. I see it as something to embrace and learn from and thank and then set aside, God willing.

Call or write as you wish or can. Don't be alarmed if you don't get me for a while, for I may end up spending some time at my parents' house, depending on the degree of help I need. Give my love to all.

The message in the basement and the one Tom found in his cancer are one and the same: we are here to generate and receive love and beauty. This message is more than the statement of a fine teacher; it is the explanatory key to the characteristics that enable someone to teach with grace. To understand anything accomplished with excellence, explanations must go beyond method and technique; we must fathom, instead, the impulses that make possible extraordinary care. The message on the blackboard points to the interplay of love and beauty. Beauty isn't that which is pleasing, nor does it lie in some formal harmony or symmetry. Too much of "the beautiful" is simply what fits societal norms and standards. Instead, beauty lies in the radiant display of the fullness and depth of persons and objects that happens only when they are loved. It is the revelation that the ordinary isn't. Fundamental to all caring is this interplay: the more one loves, the more beauty one finds; the more beauty one finds, the more one loves. To witness the grace of a teacher, we must move to that basement where the unmistakable love for one's students and the act of teaching itself is realized and grounded.

When seeking to identify good teachers, note their behavior in the everyday and, particularly, when times are hard. Observe whether they incline to basements. Pay attention to their words, but prize especially the consistency between word and act. Listen for their joy in learning (and teaching) and whether laughter rings from their classrooms. And if you find such teachers, remember them, for some people, and the gift of care they freely give us, ought not to be forgotten.

SIX

"Where Did We Go Right?"

TWO CHARACTERS IN *The Producers*,[31] MAX BIALYSTOCK and Leo Bloom, set about concocting the perfect Broadway flop. They've figured out that by overcapitalizing a surefire bomb, they can turn a handsome profit with a theatrical disaster. Despite their best intentions and considerable efforts to organize one of the worst musicals imaginable, however, their *Springtime for Hitler* actually succeeds, prompting their plaintive question: "Where did we go right?"

Unlike Max and Leo, most educators don't spend much time lamenting their successes; instead, we worry about what went wrong: Why the low scores on an exam? Why the drooping eyelids in class? Why the yawning silence in response to a question? Like many educators, I pay considerably more attention to the five negative evaluations of a course than the twenty-five that are positive. The same tendency is evident in attending to students in the back row, who constantly seem to advertise their desire to be as physically removed from class as cinderblocks will allow. Often, I focus more on their indifference than on the interested faces up front, and I'm likely not alone in doing so. I wish that I could put a bright spin on my attention to the negative by arguing that we grow from criticism, learn from our mistakes, or have a soft spot for the disaffected. Some of these rationalizations are undoubtedly true; however, in my case at least, the preoccupation is often laced with grimmer motives, like fear and self-doubt.

In this chapter, I want to pursue an alternative to these negative motives. I want to celebrate a success—to remember, in some detail, a specific course that stands out in my teaching experience as an occasion of joy—and pose to it the question from *The Producers*: what went right? This focus isn't an exercise in self-congratulation. Occasionally, and thankfully, classes go right, and if we pay attention to them, our successes may guide our future.

I offered the course during a four-week summer session in July 2001; it ran three days a week for three hours each morning and enrolled twenty-two students. The course was, in many ways, an anomaly for me. Living and working in Maine, where summers can seem a delightful blip between mud season and snowstorms, I rarely teach between June and September. Summers are my time to write and to restore my (and particularly my wife's) faith that withstanding Maine winters still makes sense. I also have a problem with condensing my regular courses into brief summer semesters. Even when class time is equivalent, the time to read and reflect between classes isn't. Four weeks a semester do not make.

So what led me to abandon my convictions? The short answer (and for those who have experienced it, I need say little more) is that my younger son was entering college. If he were to emerge without debt past his eyeballs, my principles had to bend. The one line I had drawn in the sand, though, was a refusal to complete in four weeks work that would normally take fifteen. This refusal was the last remaining shred of my rapidly tattering scruples against highly condensed summer courses. In this case, the marriage of necessity and conscience became, as the old cliché suggests, the mother of invention. The course would be an experiment—but in what sense?

For reasons I now understand in retrospect, the answer to this question was immediate: the course would be an experiment in reading. I had been struck for some time by how hypocritical, even contradictory, many courses (mine included) are in terms of an unrelenting emphasis on the coverage of material. We teach works, arguing for their historical, cultural, even spiritual importance, then undercut their purported value by asking that students read them at breakneck speed. Two weeks on Plato's *Republic*, and it's on to Aristotle's *Nicomachean Ethics*.[32] We end up encouraging a gloss, a sliding across the surface of works.

Of course, my long-standing reasons for packing courses with material were well rehearsed. But my justifications had begun to seem limp, even to me. Gaining intellectual breadth *is* important. Familiarity with diverse authors, traditions, and historical periods *does* matter. But—and this *but* is the annoying fly in the proverbial ointment—I also know that the constant emphasis on breadth results in courses that can resemble forced marches through abstract intellectual landscapes. Education that's worth its salt can never be reduced to the provision and storage of information. What matters, first and finally, is the experience of deep engagement, and such connection is impossible without patient, concentrated slowness. These convictions were longstanding, but I often struggled to enact them.

I decided to slow down dramatically. The entire course would address one book: Friedrich Nietzsche's *Thus Spoke Zarathustra*.[33] I had assigned parts of this text in other courses, but, in addition to the usual disappointment of reading only snippets of tightly woven wholes, this work seemed especially resistant to being read hastily and partially. At best, the quick reading of sections managed to whet the appetite of a few. For the overwhelming majority, however, brief dips into Zarathustra's pool were cold and disorienting. The subtitle of the work, *A Book for Everyone and No One*, often seemed to mock my forays. For everyone who hastily read portions of the work, no one (or not many) would get much out of it. Radically slowing down was an alternative to giving up on the work.

Thus Spoke Zarathustra proved an interesting choice to address the issue of reading. It doesn't mince words in pointing out that our ways of reading are problematic: "Another century of readers—and the spirit itself will stink."[34] Strewn throughout the text are comments about the kind of reading (and writing) that Nietzsche respects and others he despises. I was intrigued by the possibility of letting his remarks about reading guide our study of his text. What difference would it make? What problem(s) does Nietzsche find in our habitual type of reading, and is he correct that, unchecked and unchallenged, this manner of reading exacts a terrible price?

Like many philosophical texts, *Thus Spoke Zarathustra* has the reputation of being a very, even painfully, "heavy" text. The prospect of starting class at 8:15 every morning with its biblical (some would say bombastic) rhetoric seemed daunting, so part of the experimental aspect of the course was to find a transition into the text. I decided upon a practice that I had used privately, though never before in class, of working my way into reading philosophy through music. I decided to open the first fifteen minutes of every class (while students were putting final touches on their written responses to questions posed the previous day) by playing short musical excerpts. As this idea grew, I realized that there is a considerable body of music that is directly or indirectly concerned with Nietzsche: CDs of Nietzsche's own piano compositions that he wrote as a young man; the work of composers such as Richard Wagner, who had a major influence in Nietzsche's life; and musical compositions inspired by *Thus Spoke Zarathustra*, such as Richard Strauss' piece of the same title.[35]

I was amazed at the difference the music made. Not only did it form a bridge from the collective busyness of our mornings to the philosophical work ahead of us, it also succeeded in creating a meditative atmosphere in the class. The music seemed to induce listening. It quieted us, seeming to create a posture of stillfulness. Of course, my shuttling across campus each morning with an awkward boom box and a clutch of CDs also became a source of some ribbing from colleagues. Was I abandoning philosophy for the symphony? Had I discovered the will to music? An associate dean quipped that judging from the music streaming from the room in the early morning, I had found the classical equivalent of showing a movie in every class. "Is popcorn being offered?" he teased.

Despite the jokes about it, the music became decisive in our investigation of the text. For example, after listening to Nietzsche's piano music, one student expressed surprise that its tone was so hesitant, so subdued, almost quiet, a distinct contrast from the form she had expected: something more Wagnerian, more imperious and insistent. Her remark led to a discussion of the *tone*, the dominant mood or key, in which Nietzsche wrote *Thus Spoke Zarathustra*. We debated whether such a trait was discernible and, if so, what difference it made to our reading. Does the assertive mood of many statements mask a far more hesitant, almost quiet, attitude? Does the tone of the work change as Zarathustra undergoes his metamorphoses? This discussion opened up other questions: Does every philosophical work have a characteristic tone? To interpret a text well, must we identify the tone out of which it is written? How do we learn to listen for it? Is locating and understanding it an essential part of reading well? We also began to notice the extent to which musical imagery dominates this text, and we examined what this overt connection might mean in terms of understanding Nietzsche's thought. This link was new territory for me, and it was exciting.

At the outset of the course, the idea of making it an experiment in reading meant little more than deciding to slow down, to concentrate on only one work and go over it line by line. But this first step led to others, such as paying closer attention to remarks in the text about how it wishes to be read. An entire section in the first part of *Zarathustra* concerns reading and writing. It opens with the following lines:

> Of all that is written I love only what a man has written with his blood. Write with blood, and you will experience that blood is spirit.
>
> It is not easily possible to understand the blood of another: I hate reading idlers.[36]

Passages like this became decisive in our efforts at interpretation. Students started asking what it means for someone to write and read with blood. More than a few noted that a great deal of philosophy seems much removed from anything to do with blood and is more of a head game, an exercise in conceptual analysis. Writing with blood suggests a very different way of pursuing philosophy. It seems to posit that one's thought is intimately tied to, even guided by, the deepest substrates of the body: its instincts and drives, needs and emotions. Zarathustra claims that if philosophy is to recover its distinctive role as an initiator of spiritual transformation, it must move ever closer to what he calls "the great reason" of the body.[37]

At its best, philosophy is occupied with the broadest and deepest questions about how we relate to the world, the basic purposes and values that orient our living. If Zarathustra is correct, our relationship to the world, though certainly involving concepts and reasoning, should never be reduced to a matter of disembodied, abstract intelligence. We relate out of the depths of our instincts and drives, from the patterns of our feelings and sensitivities, our decisions and resolve: the "blood" out of which Nietzsche writes. Any philosophical work that pretends to be a matter of "cold, pure, divinely unconcerned dialectic" is not only kidding itself but is also distancing itself from the unsettling but fertile sources of spiritual development.[38] Logical argument—the reflective examination of claims and counterclaims—is, of course, important in philosophy. Nietzsche wouldn't disagree. How could we analyze our lives and thoughts if we abandoned logic and reflection? Nietzsche insists, however, that logic is never primary. Before we logically analyze anything, we participate—are actively involved—in the world: we engage in caring, make commitments, and embark upon certain projects to which we become emotionally bound.

Nietzsche characterizes traditional philosophers, who would vehemently deny his claims, as lawyers who resent the title.[39] We can approach the world as neutral, dispassionate observers only by progressively abstracting and reducing ourselves from full-bodied engagement to the point that we approximate spectral intellects (pure subjects, thinking egos). Nietzsche wonders what factors motivate this abstraction of philosophical selves and is convinced that the answer lies in a form of revenge against life. We practice such revenge in demanding certainty, permanence, and security. We turn against the ever-changing, ungraspable immensity of life, because it denies us the satisfaction and control we so deeply desire. We ask of life what it cannot provide. We make "objectivity" and "logic" the measure of thought, because we love life insufficiently.

Nietzsche's admiration for those who write with blood is indicative of how he wishes readers to engage his work. He knows that writing in blood imposes difficult demands upon readers. Part of the difficulty reflects the fact that so much of what we read is bloodless. It is "top of the head stuff," written on the surface for surface reading. Inexperienced with bloody writers, we become "reading idlers." Conversely, in Nietzsche, we encounter an author who writes from the fullness of both body and mind. We sense his anger, feel the bite of his sarcasm, hear his peals of laughter. Yet if we listen carefully, we also discover the incredible gentleness—I would go so far as to say the protective tenderness—of his desire. Consider, for example, the philosophical blessing that he offers in the text: "But this is my blessing: to stand over every single thing as its own heaven, as its round roof, its azure bell, and eternal security."[40] In contrast to so much of the philosophical tradition that tries to nail things down and, again and again, thinks it has succeeded, Nietzsche seeks to shelter what-is, to protect it by refusing to assume that anyone can intellectually encompass it. He restores its inherent strangeness.

In our dialogue about the meaning of reading idly, the class arrived at the insight that it involves inattention to the possibility that something spiritually important might be at stake in our encounter with a text. Idle reading is information gathering. It never goes beyond written words to the unspoken message that lies between them—to that space where the encounter of one human being speaking with another, depth to depth, takes place. In idle reading, we don't invest our lives; we insulate ourselves from being "bitten" by the words of another. We read impersonally, as if we've abstracted our flesh and blood existence into the status of objective observers. In idle reading, we take our own lives for granted or, in what amounts to the same, we take our selves out of play and, in so doing, undercut the possibility of dialogue. We read in a way that never puts us at risk and will, therefore, never lead to change.

Such reading is not purely a matter of personal choice. It is encouraged, and one source of encouragement is the very coverage of material that dominates higher education. Perhaps it's a matter of my own aging, but the world of the academy increasingly appears to me as hypnotically rushed, chronically busy. We seem to assume that by cramming a large number of texts into a short amount of time, we are somehow accomplishing something. Such reading will never scent the blood of another in the writing; it hasn't the time, patience, or attentiveness. Such reading does not battle texts, nor will it ever weep and dance with them. More often than not, classes "cover" readings at the same speed with which tourists take in scenic highlights—and, I'm afraid, with similar results in terms of being unaffected by the visits. Syllabi read like packaged travel tours: On Tuesday, it's *No Exit,*[41] Thursday, *The Myth of Sisyphus.*[42]

But when thoughtful contemplation and active discussion banish idle reading, as they did in this course, here is what happens: A field of electricity occurs between the pole of the students and the pole of the text. The teacher serves as a conductor, helping to make possible the jumping of the gap. The classroom comes to resemble a powerful battery, generating energy. I witnessed sparks a number of times in this course. Several factors helped make this energy possible: First, this particular text demands that people read it against the grain of their lives. Nietzsche chose to write it in a biblical style of story and aphorism that forces readers, not to a definitive conclusion, but to take its words and images into their own lives as a means of interpretation. Second, the course was fortunate to enroll a critical mass of students who were willing to both probe and be provoked by the text. Third, by sheer luck of the draw, the course attracted a mixture of students, about half of whom I already knew. It was also an "older" group; many were involved in their education for reasons beyond the dollar sign. Fourth, as soon as I could see that the dynamic interplay between the book and the class was occurring, I had the good sense to step out of the way and let it happen. I rejoined the class as a participant. Finally, the very subject matter of the text—the process of spiritual transformation—heightened our awareness that education is primarily about the delightfully messy process of growing beyond who we have been. In the text of *Zarathustra*, Nietzsche identifies the goal of education as becoming who one is. For him, we are most fully human in our capacity for creative becoming. To reclaim our creativity is to become ourselves. We achieve humanity in undertaking our own growth, even to the point of articulating new criteria for what "growth" means.

These transformations often take place in quiet, unassuming ways. The privilege of witnessing them is the thrill of teaching. Let me give a few examples from the course. One student, a middle-aged woman, described herself on the very first day as a committed feminist. Not surprisingly, she found *Thus Spoke Zarathustra* very difficult to read in terms of what it says and doesn't say about women. She had no shortage of sections, quotes, and language from which to draw. The entire text addresses itself almost exclusively to Zarathustra's "brothers." To an overwhelming extent, the figures who show up in the text—the jester, the priests, the hunchback, and tightrope walker—are male. This bias in characters and form of address is only the first layer of difficulty. There are sections, for example in "On Little Old and Young Women," where one could label Nietzsche's misogynistic statements as downright painful to encounter. The brutality of these statements has led me to wonder at times whether I should be asking my students, the majority of whom are women, to crack its covers. Here are some choice examples:

The happiness of man is: I will. The happiness of woman is: he wills. "Behold, just now the world became perfect!"—thus thinks every woman when she obeys out of entire love. And woman must obey and find a depth for her surface. Surface is the disposition of woman: a mobile, stormy film over shallow water.

This passage ends with the famously disturbing words: "Then I said: 'Woman, give me your little truth.' And thus spoke the little old woman: 'You are going to women? Do not forget the whip!'"[43]

In another section, entitled "On The Friend," Zarathustra says, "Are you a slave? Then you cannot be a friend. Are you a tyrant? Then you cannot have friends. All-too-long have a slave and a tyrant been concealed in woman. Therefore woman is not yet capable of friendship: she knows only love."[44] Statements like these tend to make one cringe, swear, or hurl the book against the nearest wall.

Early in the course, the middle-aged student to whom I referred savaged the text for its sexism and challenged the class to provide alternative interpretations of the passages that enraged her. For a long time, no one seemed willing to take up her challenge, which cast an uneasy pall over subsequent discussions of the thinker's work. By the time of her in-class presentation, however, her anger had moderated. She commented on this change herself by referencing a series of emails that she had exchanged with a classmate who had offered suggestions that opened up new interpretive possibilities. One of these suggestions was that Zarathustra's harsh words against women are some of the very same criticisms that feminists would make of nineteenth-century stereotypes of "female" behavior—stereotypes constructed by and for men. Thus, the student posited, his denigration is less an attack against women than criticism of the social roles that they have been forced to fit.

For her presentation, she had found evidence that Nietzsche was aware of and sympathetic to the plight of women, who were taught to be coy and innocent in pursuit of a husband (after which, they were expected to be sophisticated lovers and shrewd household managers). She identified that Nietzsche was a man who spent considerable time with female friends and who, while a professor in Basel, had signed unpopular petitions to admit female students and hire female professors.

I admired the fact that this student allowed such insights to complicate her view of Nietzsche and his attitude toward women. She began to consider alternative purposes that the statements might serve: were they to attack; provoke; test; or, as she initially assumed, demean? Even when she couldn't settle such questions, she still appreciated that the text refused to hide the problem of gender relations. She acknowledged that the section "On Little Old and Young Women" is torturously complex, with many of its worst comments uttered not by Zarathustra but by an old woman. She also granted that Zarathustra speaks of both life and his wisdom as female. She concluded her talk with a series of stunning perceptions (which I hastily scribbled down):

> I continue to believe that Zarathustra has a problem with women. In this sense, he is crippled. But I also see him involved in a quest to develop. I'd like to think the same of myself. For a long time, I've been trapped by my anger, my anger against men. Anger has its place, but it's time for me to go beyond it; otherwise, I just consume myself in opposition.[45]

This woman's ability—and most notably her willingness—to reconsider remarks that she hated at first was a considerable personal accomplishment. It took courage to admit her anger, not only in response to this text but also in her life generally. In a curious way, her admission of this emotion connected her to Zarathustra's struggle to deal with his own anger. I could also see (and took as a success) that the dialogue emerging in the course—for instance, in the strings of emails among classmates—was partly responsible for this transformation. Students were teaching each other, which happened because they began to care about the text and their interpretations of it. I am convinced that without the slow, unhurried reading of the text, epiphanies of this sort could not have occurred.

Another student, a devotee of the martial arts, zeroed in on Nietzsche's claim that the highest spiritual task is to become who you are. As I learned more about him from class and office visits, I recognized that a substantial portion of this young man's personality had been constructed in direct response to years of physical and sexual abuse at the hands of a stepfather. It was chilling to begin to grasp how this student would read and interpret passages in the text. For example, in a section entitled "The Tomb Song," Zarathustra revisits the "tombs" of his youth. He recalls "the visions and dearest wonders of [his] youth"—he actually calls them his "divine moments"— and how they were destroyed by his Christian upbringing:

> For you murdered the visions and dearest wonders of my youth. My playmates you took from me, the blessed spirits. In their memory I lay down this wreath and this curse. This curse against you, my enemies. For you have cut short my eternal bliss, as a tone that breaks off in a cold night. . . .
>
> Thus spoke my purity once in a fair hour: "All beings shall be divine to me." Then you assaulted me with filthy ghosts; alas, where has this fair hour fled now?
>
> "All days shall be holy to me"—thus said the wisdom of my youth once; verily, it was the saying of a gay wisdom. But

then you, my enemies, stole my nights from me and sold them into sleepless agony.[46]

Through the eyes of this student, I could begin to understand the rage behind Zarathustra's words. The young man was not claiming that Zarathustra had been sexually abused; his point was that abuse of children occurs in many ways and that any and all of them are horrifying. Because of this student, I could appreciate Zarathustra's "nights . . . sold . . . into sleepless agony" with vividness previously absent. This young man also knew such nights and was aware that abuse of any sort stunts people's development, freezing them into set, reactive postures of anger, depression, fear, avoidance, or violence.

My student helped me to see that the profundity of Zarathustra's need to "become who you are" grows out of the life-and-death struggle to move beyond the tomblike, constructed self that he built in response to what he perceives as abuse. Zarathustra seeks to recover the life-enhancing possibility of growing beyond all that is fixed and dead in him. My student was struggling to build anew a life spent cursing his stepfather, to overcome the self that he had constructed (the tough-guy persona) in response to the childhood horrors visited upon him. He started to realize that, in one form or another, the task of spiritual metamorphosis is one that all human beings face, undertake, or forego. Sadly, many lose any sense of this journey to "become" and, although it sounds strange at first, this neglect has everything to do with how we learn to read. My student was not reading to get through material but for life itself; he was "reading into" Zarathustra what the text itself calls for, namely, the willingness to put oneself on the line, to risk disturbance. He was reading for survival. For blood.

This young man's journey to confront his abuse was not completed in the course but, in it, there was already the undeniable sense that the process of facing his anger and seeking an alternative was underway. One year later (and memory of this fact still causes the hairs on the back of my neck to rise), he completed an undergraduate thesis on "A Philosophy *Toward* Forgiveness" that ended with the following lines:

> The actual experience [of learning to forgive] is deeply embedded in the particulars, the everyday discoveries, the tears, the terror, the panic attacks, the times I laughed when I found something that shed a little light. . . . But philosophy was always there; it called me to wonder, to actually take part in my own experience, to actually participate in who I am. Without philosophy, life becomes an investment in alienation and ignorance—two things that forgiveness destroys when it returns one to oneself.[47]

This student and others made teaching the course a privilege. I had the sense of teaching to that nexus where people and a great work intersect. I found students (not all of them, but enough) who were willing to read and be read with blood and, in watching them wrestle with this text, rediscovered the immense power that a philosophical work holds, waiting to be tapped. It may sound strange for a professor of philosophy to admit to this discovery, but I think that teachers, like everyone else, go through periods when we take our work for granted and become somewhat blasé about the life-changing capacity of the texts we use and the way we teach. This course reawakened my conviction that in teaching, lives are at stake.

I wish I could say that the course's success was a matter of deliberate planning, but it wasn't. Much of its good fortune depended upon accidental factors, as I've tried to show: the make-up of the class, the spot decision to use music. The credit I will take is that I was ready and willing to depart from many long-engrained teaching habits and try something new. I moved toward a more personal encounter with a text and my students. Neither disappointed. The students grasped that the way to understand *Thus Spoke Zarathustra* had to be through the struggle to understand themselves.

My reflection on "What went right?" doesn't conclude that this course was a model. At that point, it would merely become another habit. Although I basked in the opportunity it presented to concentrate on one work, I wouldn't advocate an education from which breadth, in favor of depth, is excluded. There are risks and weaknesses in reading so personally and so focally. It's important to approach works in broader contexts and to test our personal responses with secondary commentary and critical theory. But in its time and context, the course was right. It helped me to restore a balance to my work as a teacher and provided something that Max Bialystock and Leo Bloom discovered as well: After lamenting the success of their play and the possibility of a long prison stay for filching its financial backers, the two sing a concluding number. "Prisoners of Love" is a song about friendship, a recognition that what makes (in their case) success and the prospect of prison bearable are the relationships that people build. This creation of connection took place that summer in 2001.

The fact that relationships formed in this course has much to do with the resolve to address the issue of reading. In the section "On Reading and Writing," to which I earlier referred, there occurs one of the most powerful lines for me in the entire book: "We are all of us fair beasts of burden, male and female asses. What do we have in common with the rosebud,

which trembles because a drop of dew lies on it?"⁴⁸ I won't go
into all of my reasons for finding this line so beautiful. Suf-
fice it to say that for an author who is so renowned for his
strident personality, for his willingness to philosophize with a
hammer, it is striking that he asks this question of himself and
others: "What do we have in common with the rosebud?" It is
a question of incredibly delicate tenderness that imagines the
possibility of a human life trembling because of a dewdrop.

Though I loved the line, I had never pushed my understanding of it further. In the final paper for the course, the
"tough guy" wrote the following while addressing a point
about how frightening change can be:

> "What do we have in common with the rosebud, which
> trembles because a drop of dew lies on it?" First off, what we
> have in common is that like the flower, we are the potential
> of a beautiful thing just waiting to burst forth in all our
> splendor. The rose is one of those great symbols in the world
> that, time and again, represents life and the complexity of
> the individual in the unfolding of all its promise.
>
> Why does the rose tremble from a drop of dew? What is
> dew but the stuff of morning nourishment for plants, that
> which refreshes them and encourages them to grow? That
> drop of dew on the rosebud is our first taste of the kind of
> wisdom that forces us to face our growth; it is the sweetness
> of life, and to the unfulfilled, it is terrifying. What we have
> in common with the bud is now we, too, have been given
> the first drop of nourishment and now we must face the
> day.⁴⁹

This is the kind of reading that I believe Nietzsche would
respect and is one of the reasons I remember the course so

fondly. My remembrance, however, is not simply a recalling of the past. Memory opens up a future by allowing something cherished to bring a smile and confidence that, on occasion, and beyond our planning, things can go utterly right.

SEVEN

Two Sticks of Bare Leg

ॐ

AS PROMISED, THIS BOOK OFFERS NO BLUEPRINT
for educational reform, nor any list of techniques for the improvement of teaching. It concentrates, instead, on the actual experience of teaching through the medium of stories.
In conclusion, though, I'd like to stand back from the stories
and sift them for underlying themes. If transformation lies at
the heart of teaching, can we gain insight into this alchemical process? How do we invite and encourage it? What factors promote transformation? What aspects hinder it? There's
no formula for engineering transformation (the variables are
at once too vast and too particular), but there are, I believe,
underlying patterns in its occurrence, certain attitudes and
actions conducive to its possibility.

The material for this book didn't emerge from any conscious plan. Rather, the pieces formed as I paid attention to events of change in classrooms—occurrences that shaped my sense of students and myself as a teacher. I wrote them originally as memory devices, experiences that I wanted to put on paper in response to the nagging thought, *you'd better not forget this.* As stories piled up, I noticed how many of them focused on individual students: Emma, Mildred, Darwin, Darcy. In retrospect, this focus on individuals shouldn't be surprising. The awareness that distinguishes teaching from instruction fundamentally involves mindfulness of the people in our midst—those two sticks of bare leg that my sister affixed to her office door. Upon watchfulness for unfolding lives, everything else depends.

Ultimately, lives depend on it. Some academics argue that this assumption is narcissistic and attributes far too much power and influence to educators. It assumes, they claim, that educators know better than the students themselves about which transformations are desirable for students and which are not.[50]

I understand the caution. The demand that students change according to a teacher's plan is a terrible directive to impose. Moreover, my sense is that no such decree is necessary. As the French writer Anaïs Nin once wrote, "Life is a process of becoming, a combination of states we have to go through. Where people fail is that they wish to elect a state and remain in it. This is a kind of death."[51] We teachers are involved in the alteration of lives not because we demand it, but because students are engaged in change whether we like it or not. We can assist the change by sparking awareness of it. We can help students acknowledge the importance and dynamics of their own growth. We can give encouragement and suggestion. We can lead students into contact with authors who underwent similar struggles. Human change is, in fact, seldom accomplished by oneself. It emerges, for better or worse, from the involvement of others. Participation in such transformation is one of the great delights and responsibilities of teaching.

Transformation fundamentally involves a change of consciousness, and for teachers to have any intentional effect on consciousness, we must be acutely aware of students—their thoughts and values, attitudes and emotions, fears and hopes. This belief is easy to verbalize but difficult to achieve, because indications of their lives are often fleeting and masked: the quiet withdrawal, a nervous smile, hasty words in the office, the missing assignment. The signs are easy to overlook, as Bruegel shows in his painting. We're engrossed in our tasks. We think that there are more important matters. We can find it easier and less time consuming to turn away. Environments that don't value teaching often reward people for concentrating on other activities. Neglect of the minute events of everyday life occurs for many reasons. But if teaching centrally concerns a change of consciousness, then paying careful attention to both students and oneself is imperative and nonnegotiable.

The question, of course, is how. The ways are endless and include tending to the simple gesture of learning students' names or trying to listen better, growing bigger ears. Educators enact such care in having the time to talk and the patience to be silent, in the observance of faces, in the willingness to alter plans in order to better engage the students in one's midst. Attention flows from the realization that teaching demands this awareness and that few actions are more important. Care is evident in the design of classes and assignments through which students can make themselves known. Teaching works to create an environment wherein change is possible. It's to the construction of place that I would now like to turn.

A Space for Recognition

It seems to me that one, if not *the*, defining purpose of classrooms is that they're spaces dedicated to human development. I find this belief definitive—it shapes everything else. Stated this baldly, however, the connection between space and human development is so abstract as to seem useless. But it can be unpacked. One meaning is that the learning environment cannot be crammed so tightly with information and instruction (literally, the building *in* of material) that there's little or no place for persons. For transformation to be possible, we must attend to our own awareness and encourage its interaction with that of others. In short, classrooms must be places that encourage students (and teachers) to be present. They must preserve room for the unsolicited response; the stifled question; the unanticipated connection; the expression of frustration and boredom; the pause to reconsider; and, if one is lucky, the occasional whoop of joy. They must invite students—repeatedly—to be alert to and engaged with their own learning. This engagement is impossible when teaching is narrowly and primarily focused on the transference of information. I may be banned from the online community for saying so, but attention to the environment of teaching demands concern for its physical dimension as well.

People can be instructed (furnished with information) without being educated. Education is tougher. It goes beyond the transfer of data to a search for its meaning, to the consideration of how and by whom the information will be used, the purposes behind it and those it will serve, as well as active examination of the data's limits. All of these functions require freedom of movement—the ability to go beyond the fixity of fact. The key to sustaining this movement is recognition of those legs—the awareness that, ultimately, we're teaching people, not subjects. Certain ways of preserving space depend upon circumstances. For example, although I'm chronically "old school" in my reluctance to use class time for showing movies, I know the importance that film holds for students and have developed the practice of incorporating an evening film series into my upper-level philosophy courses. The series is optional. I bribe students with popcorn. But the conversations about the films have proven, time and again, invaluable. Because there's no fixed agenda and no one is leading the discussion, students talk differently than they do in the formal environment of a class. I learn about their lives. I have the chance to hear what's on their minds and can gauge whether and how the material we're studying speaks to their concerns. One learns that the nexus between lives and subjects is not simply intellectual but a matter of the imagination and the emotions as well.

A final reason why classrooms must preserve space for people to be present is simply this: teaching depends on it. This statement isn't hyperbole. If teaching is fundamentally about human transformation, then without opportunities to develop knowledge of and affection for one's students, teachers undergo burnout. They turn into creatures of another sort: instructors, publishing phenoms, theatrical performers, or military police. Like any service profession, teachers can come to resent the very neediness of students that brings them to school in the first place. Anyone familiar with faculty lounges knows the war stories of student stupidity, the jokes told at students' expense, the slow refusal to care, the perfunctory comments on papers—in short, the decay of teaching into sheer habit, the living death of merely going through the motions.

This decay is difficult to address. One can't be ordered to care. When administrators or colleagues try, these educational zombies find ways around the orders and substitute pretense for substance. Nor can people force *themselves* to care. Care isn't a function of willpower; for it to arise, relationship must form, as only it makes possible appreciation and a sense of connection. Conversely, carelessness results from isolation. For this reason, one of the only defenses against teacher burnout is the opportunity to know and engage students. Of course, such relation will never be all sweetness and light. It will entail dealing with comatose clods, clever fakers, and manipulative climbers—the usual broad and disturbing range of humanity. In my experience, however, students will more often surprise one with their decency than disappoint one with its lack.

Interestingly, as stories in this book accumulated, a direction made itself apparent without any intention on my part. The theme of contact with students expresses itself consistently in terms of a going down, of moving below the surface. Tom left his message in a basement. Plato describes education as taking place in a cave that teachers must enter. Teachers speak (properly, I think) of being "in the trenches"—a telling metaphor combining battle imagery with a life-saving proximity to the ground. Both senses are apropos. They capture the struggle and physicality of any close human involvement. As I suggested in "Teaching Babel," working with Darwin often triggered the feeling of hand-to-hand combat. The Shaker song in "Among Small Beauties" tells of learning to bow and bend in the *valley* of love and delight. The description of Emma's "meltdown" was terribly apt. Perhaps the closer we come to life, to actual lived experience, grappling with an earthy grubbiness is inescapable. So, too, in teaching, especially when it's occupied with human transformation. Hands must get dirty insofar as we can't distance ourselves from those we teach. Transformation, as the occurrence of conscious change, is both a messy struggle and (lest we forget) something lovely. Such teaching takes place in the trenches, the mud and slog, the chaos of the human—a landscape avoided by supervisors and field generals.

One final point about teaching's inclination to the "down and dirty": this orientation is often demeaned. We praise the move upward, the climb to the top, the view from above. We like the clarity, simplicity, and loftiness of the bird's-eye perspective, in part, for its distance from the confusing messiness below. Height often implies status and achievement, being a cut above the rest. These attitudes clearly affect teaching. In colleges and universities, for example, it's common to distinguish "teaching loads," from "research opportunities." The choice of words is telling. Movement "up the ladder" in academia is often associated with distance from students or, at least, from the great unwashed in introductory general-education courses. Unfortunately, this preference for moving above rather than toward the trenches often entails a diminution of the act of teaching itself.

But the worst forms of deprecation are self-inflicted; teachers, if we're not careful, receive a great deal of help in forgetting the importance of our own work and grow to regard it as somehow less significant than that of managers and administrators. We risk internalizing the terrible judgment that "Those who can—do. Those who can't—teach."[52] Such words ravage any sense of teaching as a noble act. In place of teach-ing, educators emulate and glorify other roles: the gifted re-searcher, the administrative powerhouse, the conference hot shot—almost anyone other than that person in the classroom.

I don't wish to polarize teaching and scholarship, both of which can and should inform one another. Nor do I seek to separate teaching from other collegial and professional obli-gations. Ultimately, however, the balance must work to serve the students in our care.

Of course, the involvement of teachers with students is affected not only by internal attitudes but also by external factors. For example, the number of students in classes dra-matically affects a teacher's ability to form relationships with students. For every teacher, there's a figure beyond which it's extremely difficult to expect any clear sense of the persons with whom one is working. I can't say what that number is for others. But even in the worst of lecture-hall scenarios, there are always ways, however restricted, to invite one's audience to make themselves known—if only to take special care and, hence, time for question and response.

Another constraint on maintaining a place for the per-sonal is that many courses require the heavy transmittal of information. Course X is a prerequisite for course Y, and the latter presupposes that students possess a certain knowledge base and have required skills. Such fields and disciplines are so highly specialized that imagining room for the personal is very difficult. If so, what to do?

I'd like to make several points about these cases. First, the provision of information isn't itself the problem. Information provides a necessary and fruitful ground for question and re-flection. Rather, the problem is insistence upon information without corresponding attention to the context that frames the information, the question(s) to which the information is a response, and how students will use the information. Information without mindfulness of the larger context from which it emerged and that to which it will go is a false and dangerous privileging of data.

Second, even where provision of information and skill formation is imperative, inattention to the learner proves counterproductive. Without opportunities for teachers to address why certain information is necessary or for students to question the emphasis upon "facts and their regurgitation," there is a petrifaction of education into data transfer and learning into a commodity.

Third, when courses are so weighted in terms of prescribed data that they foreclose opportunities for broader questions and considerations, teachers need to step back and reexamine whether coverage of material is diminishing learning.

These considerations hold even in nonliterary disciplines. Consider, for example, the study of mathematics. Many students in the humanities have a phobia about math. They avoid elective courses in it like cafeteria food and will often postpone mandatory ones until absolutely the last moment. One reason for this dread is that, over previous years of schooling, no one seriously addressed the issue of what mathematics is or its uses and necessity. No one examined math as a symbolic order of the human mind and a tool of inquiry for organizing and understanding experience. My point is that, even here, where one might least expect it, there is need to engage imagination and the demand for meaning. When teachers introduce math with no sense of its need, connection, and meaning, it becomes, for some, deadening—a set of static formulas for passing exams that is useless in lived experience.

Students will cue us, if we listen, to obstacles they're facing, to assumptions and practices that undercut their interest. They'll let us know, if we pay attention, when connections spark, when points hit home. Heads raise. Bodies move forward. Pupils widen. Conversely, students convey indifference just as articulately. They'll sometimes freely dispense this information; other times, teachers must solicit it. For example, I've developed the habit of asking students at the start of class why they think I chose a particular reading or assignment, and what they thought of it. These open-ended questions direct students' attention back to their own learning. Their responses also clue me in to operative assumptions that may obstruct their learning. I was amazed in an introductory philosophy class, for example, to learn of a student's dismissal of material because it had been written centuries before. Old, to this student, meant outdated. But once the idea was out on the table, we could address it. I remember kidding the class that philosophers must have either a very high tolerance for ancient material or very low expectations for relevance. We then launched into a discussion of when and why historical material is relevant, and whether part of the ability of certain texts to challenge our assumptions could stem from the fact that they come from times and cultures so different from our own. The discussion was a departure from the day's plan but, without it, some students would have quickly dismissed the analysis of ancient material as little more than an unnecessary museum trip.

The Provocation of Wonder

Another theme in these stories is the need to create interest in subjects. The point sounds utterly obvious: without interest, nothing is well attended. Yet if this point is so evident, why does academia so often overlook it? Substitutes for interest—the quick pep talk, the extra-credit option, periodic instructional tantrums about the listlessness of students—all fail in the long run.

Teachers must find ways to show information as worthy of thought, as provocative, questionable, or disturbing. Instead of being the simplest and most elementary of tasks, this undertaking is among the most difficult, especially because the job isn't to reveal one's own interest in a subject, but to tap that of students. Telling students that they should be interested is beside the point. Uncovering their interest is the goal.

Examples of this mission occur in the stories, for example, when Emma discovers that Plato's myth of the cave concerns her own situation, or when Darcy finds elements of herself in Louisa. Realizing that the story of Babel might speak against his certainties is what piqued Darwin's engaged disquiet. The Nietzsche course proved successful because it asked students to read an author who is openly suspicious of them as readers. Students were led to confront themselves by an author who annoyed and frustrated their usual ways of approaching a text. He demanded that they read for blood—theirs' and his.

The point is finding ways for learning to rebound upon the learner. It's a matter of locating interest. Numerous questions surround the importance of interest in learning: Do we presume interest? Do we assume that it has been fostered elsewhere? Do we consider it someone else's job? My thinking is that we need to define what we mean by the term *interest* and the phrase *getting students to be interested*. We often conceive of interest like an arrow of attention that we shoot at some object. Taken as such, interest resides within us. It's under our control and only a matter of decision to employ it. We have interest or we don't. We *make* something interesting. I suspect, however, that this sense of interest is superficial, and the etymology of the word suggests why. *Interest* comes from two words: *inter*, meaning "between or among," and *esse*, meaning "to be." To be interested is to be in the midst of something. To be interested is to be affected or, as we say colloquially, to be grabbed by something. Interest is less like an arrow we release than a pull or a claim that someone or something exerts upon us. It's a matter of relationship that centrally concerns education, as interest is the drawing forth of something in us through contact with another. In short, *educare*. The initiation and deepening of interest is one of teaching's great tasks. To teach well is to lead students to be in the midst of a subject, and we cannot make this possible for others unless it is our own position. To educate well, we must be engaged—deeply—in the subject we teach. Interest grows as a field of study affects us on deeper and deeper levels and, for this "affection" to occur, certain rules of engagement apply. For example, very little can impinge upon us when we are speeding by it. For interest to develop, a radical slowing down must occur. I hesitate to think how often I've violated this premise. The rushed treatment of works violates the possibility of stirred interest. Moreover, in glossing over a topic or subject, students can't engage it carefully enough to recognize its value themselves. We tell them that the work is important; we don't lead them to discover it.

Deep interest derives from a peculiar emotional experience, the proper name for which is wonder. Wonder, I believe, is one of the most neglected experiences in the promotion of good teaching. This lack shouldn't be surprising, given that wonder is a disposition also widely neglected in contemporary life. In our fast-paced world, we're too busy to wonder.

We crowd it out of our thinking, our daily lives, and, unsurprisingly, our education.

Even our awareness of wonder itself grows hazy. The word has been used to cover so many varied experiences that it has undergone a kind of verbicide—the killing of any definite meaning. Ironically, the emptier of meaning it becomes, the more it is appropriated by advertisers marketing everything from the glitter of casinos to the satisfaction of purchasing fresh produce and luxury cars. We in education still toss around the term but, for the most part, as a kind of commencement piety—something to which we genuflect without real understanding of it. We celebrate wonder without stopping to think about it.

I consider wonder one of the basic dispositions of learning (and, hence, of teaching). But we often conflate wonder with experiences of curiosity and astonishment, awe and amazement. We say, for example, "I wonder where my friend is tonight" or "I wonder which team will win." In such cases, wonder is synonymous with a mild attack of curiosity. We also use the term to suggest amazement: "I stand in wonder at the Grand Canyon." In this meaning, something overwhelms a person with its special qualities—its size, complexity, age, etc. Similarly, we admire someone as wonderful: the athlete, the musical virtuoso, the mathematical genius. Note in these examples (and they're but samples) how wonder shifts from a verb to an adjective, from a particular way of being in the world to the prepackaged designation of a person or object as extraordinary.

I sense that wonder is significantly different from curiosity, astonishment, and admiration. Before trying to characterize this difference conceptually, consider an example from the stories within. Take the description of when I finished reading

Mildred's story of her mom: "Almost instinctively, I raised a hand to cover my mouth and held my breath, knowing that I had witnessed something powerful, deep, and good." That response, I believe, was one of wonder. But what are its signs? The characteristic response to moments of wonder is the sense of being stunned, that sudden arrest that leaves us unsure of what to say or do. Wonder paralyzes our normal dealings with the world. It arrests us. What accounts for this paralysis is, I think, the realization that something we presumed to know is other and more than we thought. In wonder, something breaks in upon us, as if we're encountering it for the first time. Wonder is unsettling. Not only do we confront something that we presumed to know as different and unexpected, we also realize our immense capacity for taking things for granted. Herein lies the difference of wonder from amazement and awe. In experiences of the latter, we focus on something set aside as special, as out of the ordinary. In wonder, however, something ordinary shows itself to be extraordinary. Reading Mildred's story of her mom, I had a sense of underestimating and under-appreciating the student I thought I knew. The recognition that "I had no idea" accounts for placing my hand over my mouth. Wonder stuns us into silent recognition, as our ordinary awareness is suddenly conspicuous and shows itself inadequate to grasp the person or object we have encountered.

I've heard wonder described in big words as a state of "ontological sea-sickness," in which our awareness of something's essence—its being—becomes unsettled, and this realization forces us to encounter it anew.[53] In wonder, our knowledge of something or someone proves unstable. Characteristic of this state is the sense, "I don't know what I'm dealing with." In contrast, curiosity is a state in which we seek further information about something we already presume to know. One drives by a car accident and looks to see more. One hears tidbits of an office scandal and hopes to glean further information. Both are examples of curiosity. Whereas curiosity seeks further information (more of the juicy, gory details), wonder occurs in the realization that we don't know what we thought we did. Wonder challenges our fundamental assumptions about the other and gives rise to basic questions of meaning; curiosity does not. I don't want to push these distinctions too far. There is, I think, a continuum in which curiosity and astonishment begin to intimate wonder, where the precise line between wonder and these other states is difficult to settle. My concern here is to suggest that wonder is often the medium of transformation and that a great deal of teaching leads to the provocation of wonder. As students realize that they don't know what they thought they knew, as they sense that prior assumptions are prejudices that they can overcome, as they're seized with the awareness that the object of their examination is more and different than they'd thought, wonder dawns in its terrible beauty.

The Need for Imagination

Another theme evident in these stories is the role of imagination in teaching. In "Darcy and the Red Sox," I discuss at length imagination being a central feature of human life. Here I want to address the specific role of imagination in teaching, because I believe that it's a neglected feature in the educational landscape.

In nearly every course I teach, I make use of imaginative literature. I begin my introduction to philosophy with Tolstoy's *The Death of Ivan Ilyich*.[54] Addressing the topic of friendship in a senior seminar, I use the contemporary novel *The Kite*

Runner in conjunction with otherwise straightforward philosophical texts.[55] My course in existentialism works with Sartre's plays and *The Plague* by Camus.[56] Even in courses on ancient Greek philosophy, I feature dialogues such as the *Republic* and *Symposium*, which are deeply dramatic works.[57] In short, my use of imaginative literature is a regular ploy. The question is why.

I can't say how the practice first developed—perhaps just from a love of literature on my part. It was also probably a way to break up and enliven otherwise dry, theoretical works. Whatever its origin, I use imaginative literature now for more developed reasons. Literature is immensely helpful in showing how topics and subject matter bear upon the lives of people. It takes up issues in a full-bodied manner, showing how they impact different people on emotional, conceptual, and social ways. For example, in my introductory course in philosophy, I want to address the issue of the unreflective life. What does it mean to lead such a life? How is it sustained? What are its costs? The advantage of using *The Death of Ivan Ilyich* as a wedge into this topic is that it grapples with these questions in the context of a particular person's life (or, perhaps more accurately, his death). The questions become real—almost oppressively so—as the consequences of an unexamined life spill forth into the main character's relationships with his birth family, children, wife, and colleagues. For my purposes, this personification is critical. I want students to consider something more than a theoretical point. I want them to witness the terrifying costs of an unreflective existence. I want them to not only ponder these consequences but, if possible, to recognize and feel them in lived experience.

Trying to persuade students to talk about this issue in their lives, particularly at the beginning of a course, would not only be impossible but would also inappropriately force them to discuss something personal in a public forum with strangers. Yet to initiate self-reflection, something personal must be tapped. How to achieve this personal inquiry in a class of forty? How to respect the privacy of those involved? We can't underestimate that transformation is, as Dostoevsky once said of love in action, "a harsh and dreadful thing."[58] We're dealing with a metamorphic process that, precisely because it demands change, even sacrifice, for its sake, is one that we resist.

Part of the power of imaginative stories is that they open up the personal. They illuminate specific circumstances and conditions of lived experience, yet they do so in a mediated fashion that doesn't require students to immediately confront the frightening prospect of talking about themselves and their experiences. Stories access the personal without thrusting private lives into the public sphere. With stories, students know that they're studying a life—often a life surprisingly like their own—not an abstraction, but there is some distance (however close the story may strike) between the work of fiction and themselves.

Stories also speak more fully to students than argument alone. They present thick or fat contexts, thereby resisting the possibility of being handled as mere intellectual objects. Well-told stories take hold of people's feelings and bodies. Certainly, the intellect is active in any good work of imaginative literature—skills of comparison, analysis and synthesis, and generalization are at work. But with stories, the intellect is not abstracted from other elements of the personality. Quite simply, good stories draw us in and engage us fully. As the philosopher Martha Nussbaum argues, "The particularity, the emotive appeal, the absorbing plottedness, the variety and indeterminacy, of good fiction make the reader a participant and friend."[59]

I'm not making an argument for replacing other educational texts (essays, philosophical arguments, or compilations of research data) with works of imaginative literature. Rather, I'm suggesting that the latter has a more significant role within education than the academy generally recognizes. Particularly when teaching is concerned with grabbing students' attention, with drawing them into topics that have the power to change them, this kind of literature has an important place. In many ways, these works—that treasure trove of great novels, dramas, myths, and stories in and from so many cultures—are fundamentally stories of human transformation. They may not be the only tools of alchemical teaching, but they are essential ones.

Daedalus

This book began with the painting *Landscape with the Fall of Icarus*. I'd like to end by coming back to it from a different angle. At the outset, my attention was on Icarus as he plunged into the sea. Now, in conclusion, I want to consider someone who doesn't appear in the painting but is very much in its background. That figure is Daedalus, father of Icarus.

Daedalus was a renowned inventor, craftsman, and architect in ancient Athens—a mythological Leonardo DaVinci. Among the inventions attributed to him are the axe, awl, and bevel.[60] Some mythological accounts credit him with the discovery of images. Famed for his technical innovations, Daedalus was also a renowned teacher—and it is in that realm that stories of Daedalus become darker and more complicated.

Early in his career, Daedalus was accused of murdering one of his pupils in a fit of jealous rage, fearing that the young man's invention of the saw might eclipse his own. Daedalus was arrested, put on trial, and convicted but managed to flee to Crete. There the Cretan King Minos soon recognized his talents.

King Minos had just ascended to the throne after having been granted a sign from the gods (that he, not his brother, should be king) in the form of a great, white bull. Minos promised to sacrifice the bull back to the gods but, struck by its magnificence, decided to keep it for himself and substituted another. The gods were not amused. They punished Minos by making his wife, Pasiphåe, fall in love with the beast. According to mythology, Daedalus assisted Pasiphåe by designing a wooden cow in which she hid to couple with the bull. The result of the union was the Minotaur—a fearsome creature: half man, half bull.

Daedalus' connection with the monster went deeper. King Minos, fearing both the Minotaur and the disclosure of his original greed, ordered the construction of an enormous Labyrinth in which to hide the beast. Daedalus was its architect. Eventually, the Labyrinth became a tomb for groups of young Athenians, whom King Minos regularly fed to the Minotaur out of revenge for his son being killed while visiting Athens.

Here the story intersects with the tale of the Athenian hero Theseus. Having volunteered to go as a sacrificial captive to Crete, Theseus secretly decided to kill the Minotaur. Upon his landing in Crete, Ariadne, daughter of King Minos, saw the young Athenian and fell madly in love with him. When she appealed to Daedalus for a way to protect him, Daedalus gave her a clew of thread so that Theseus could wind his way in and out of the maze and fight the Minotaur with some hope of escape. The plan worked. Theseus killed the monster and, with Ariadne, sailed to Naxos.

King Minos shut Daedalus and Icarus in a tower as punishment for his role in the Minotaur's death, but the ever-clever Daedalus fashioned wings for Icarus and himself from feathers, string, and wax. While preparing for take-off, Daedalus instructed his son to fly neither too high, because the sun's heat would melt the wax, nor too low, because sea foam would soak the feathers. As we know, Icarus failed to follow this sage advice, flew near the sun, and plummeted to his death. Daedalus, the myth reports, winged his way to Sicily, where he built a temple to Apollo, abandoned his wings, and ended up cursing all that he had achieved, because his son had died as a result of his ingenuity.

Considering the story now, I'm aware of themes that I wasn't when I first looked at the painting. I see that the myth is deeply concerned with the relation between parents and children, one generation and the next. It's also very much a myth about teaching, asking adults to consider the knowledge that they bequeath to the young. Further, the story concerns the powers and limits of technical knowledge. Daedalus is a brilliantly clever man; in fact, his very name comes from the Greek word *Daidalos*, meaning "cunning worker." In many ways, he personifies human technological inventiveness. Yet the myth repeatedly suggests that this acumen can be dangerous, even destructive. Daedalus' talents helped to procreate the Minotaur. He let tyrants employ his gifts for sinister purposes. He constructed the Labyrinth, only to have it become a slaughterhouse for the young. He mastered the principles of flight and created wings, succeeding in bringing about the death of his son.

In the background of *The Fall of Icarus*, I now see Daedalus as a failed teacher and parent. In both roles, his legacy is complex and twisted. His technological brilliance and creativity are undeniable, yet they culminate in achievements that he ends up cursing. His gifts create suffering for himself and others. His care for his son seems limited to the provision of technological devices. Is the myth a criticism of technical inventiveness? I doubt it. Whether exemplified in Labyrinths or Towers of Babel, the impulses to design and make are deeply ingrained in our human make-up and deserving of celebration. To me, the myth hints at a more subtle criticism—one that concerns education—that the transfer of technological knowledge and skills is insufficient. Technology, if we are not to rue it, must conjoin with the cultivation of humanity.

My attention shifts from those disappearing legs to the brilliant sun dominating the landscape, and the figures of the peasants going about their work. These peasants (whom Breugel often celebrates) possess something often forgotten in the midst of technological brilliance. They, frequently perforce, remain close to the Earth. In their farming, fishing, and sailing, they rely upon and care for it. Of course, they use technology as well—they harness sail and plow and fishing pole. But their tools seem observant of nature, working with its rhythms. The peasant figures seem in the landscape part of nature, not its masters. Did Breugel think that they possess a wisdom that Daedalus and his son lack? In the simplicity of their lives, do they remain faithful to the Earth, cultivating a sense of interdependence (and, hence, an awareness of limits) that neither Daedalus nor Icarus exhibit? Like the circus troupe in *Hard Times*, do these peasants possess a respect for the Earth that, for all his brilliance, Daedalus fails to teach?

This sixteenth-century painting is particularly appropriate to the world we inhabit. We're a scientific, technological culture to an extent never previously imagined. We're descendants of Daedalus. I look at those two sticks of bare leg now and confront a warning and a teaching imperative: Cultivate the humanity of the young or the advancement of technology will do us little good and considerable harm. Help them be more mindful of themselves and others. Grow compassion. Consider and make teaching a noble profession. Perhaps there's time to develop a more acute sense of the interdependence of life. Perhaps we can become more faithful to the Earth. It is for us as it was for Daedalus: the lives of our children depend on it.

Reading Group Guide

One of my hopes is that this book might serve as a springboard for conversation among teachers within reading groups or teaching improvement circles. The following questions are offered as catalysts to that end. While the questions focus on teachers, please keep in mind that my use of this term is broader than those officially certified as such. A teacher is anyone who consciously undertakes the development of another person's awareness. Parents, grandparents, coaches, friends, and colleagues often fulfill this role—sometimes in more significant ways than those at the head of classrooms.

Introduction

1. What would you post on the door of your office that would offer a glimpse into how you conceive teaching?
2. In your opinion, has the function of education shifted from the "making of lives" to the "making of livings?" What accounts for this shift? What are its consequences?

3. How would you respond to those who argue that education should not presume to transform people's lives—that such an aim, even if achievable, is arrogant and presumptuous?
4. Do you agree with the author that "Knowledge without personal development can be catastrophic?" If so, what examples would you offer to illustrate the point?
5. In your own teaching and learning were there specific incidents that whispered "Don't forget this"? What prompted these calls for remembrance?

Chapter One: Emma's Cave

1. Would you agree that "moments of real teaching often resemble debacles"? If so, why the resemblance?
2. Have you ever experienced a situation similar to Emma's, where a student breaks down in class? How did you handle it and how does it compare with the way the narrator responds to Emma?
3. This chapter offers an example of a teacher not only being taught by a student but being instructed about the importance of teaching itself. Have you had comparable experiences where a student reawakened you to the act of teaching?
4. Much of this story focuses on emotions that are in play in classrooms, in this case, fear and anxiety. Examine the role of emotions in the unfolding of this story. What is the place of emotions in the learning context?
5. It is said in this chapter that students often don't realize their roles in and responsibility for the occurrence of good teaching. Is it important that they gain this awareness? How could teachers help students be more aware of their contributions to it?

Chapter Two: Teaching Babel

1. Have you ever locked horns with a "student from hell?" Describe the experience. Did it teach you anything special?
2. If the story of Babel is interpreted as this chapter suggests, it has clear implications for those who think they know the "truth" of the Bible, for example, that the Bible itself counsels against presumptions of certainty. Why, then, do many readers of the

Bible miss this message? Do you have a different interpretation of the Tower of Babel story?

3. Do you consider Darwin's withdrawal from the course a teaching failure?
4. Are "students from hell" important instructors? In what ways?
5. Controversial material often generates heated responses that press the boundary between encouraging disagreement and maintaining respect. Do you think Darwin crosses that line? How would you have handled the challenges he presented?

Chapter Three: Darcy and the Red Sox

1. Much of this chapter concerns the role of imagination in education, arguing that it is more central than we ordinarily recognize. Do you agree? Some people would say that the importance of imagination depends on the subject, for example, that imagination might be less central in mathematics or biology than in literature or philosophy. Do you consider this a valid objection?
2. The author describes an internal debate in response to Darcy's request to postpone her presentation. Do you recognize different teaching "voices" within yourself? Try to imagine their dialogue in relation to this case.
3. "A passionate intelligence cannot take root in the transfer of information alone." What are your reasons for agreeing or disagreeing with this claim?
4. The narrator links imagination to the cultivation of compassion. What is their connection?
5. Why is Darcy's recognition that "Louisa is me" so powerful in terms of her own learning? Have you experienced similar experiences in your own education?
6. To what degree should a teacher allow a student the benefit of a "safety wink"? Would you agree that the narrator makes the right judgment in allowing Darcy to decide if she wants to present at another time? How do you distinguish between instances when such lenience is helpful and when it harms a student?

Chapter Four: Mildred

1. Have you ever found yourself caught in the ethical gray area of allowing a student an extension on an exam that was not allowed to other students? Do you think that the narrator acted rightly in offering the extension to Mildred? On what basis?

2. Motivation is critical in any learning endeavor, yet we often try to generate it through external rewards or punishments. In contrast, Mildred taps a powerful, internal drive for completing her degree. Can you suggest any ways to translate Mildred's experience more broadly into classrooms such that more students could discover depth motivations for their work?

3. Mildred's presence in the introductory philosophy course made a significant difference to it. Of course, her influence stemmed partly from her personality but also from her age. Does this story suggest that cross-generational learning ought to be pursued more broadly and robustly in education?

4. The significance of Mildred's obtaining a Bachelor's Degree only became apparent to the narrator after he learned of her family history. In your opinion, is it necessary to pay close attention to the details of students' personal lives in their education? Can you think of criticisms that might arise from giving this kind of attention to students? How might you balance intimacy and professional distance?

Chapter Five: Among Small Beauties

1. This chapter keys on an instance that, for the narrator, encapsulates the excellence of a teacher. Among fine teachers that you have known, were there particular acts that embodied their quality as teachers? Did you recognize the significance of these acts at the time of their occurrence or only in hindsight?

2. "What characterizes people who teach with genuine grace?" is the guiding question of this story. How would you answer the question for yourself? How do your responses compare to those in this chapter?

3. This chapter begins by describing Tom's personality and links it to his abilities as a teacher. Does this emphasis on his person-

ality diminish or downplay the cultivation of formal teaching techniques? Describe in some detail the personal characteristics of someone you consider an excellent teacher. How crucial are these to that person's ability to teach well?

4. The ability to listen is often celebrated, as it is in the chapter, as a mark of an accomplished teacher. What does it involve? How is this ability to listen cultivated? Why is it relatively rare to encounter an accomplished listener? Is listening a casualty of the modern age?

5. Some of this chapter revolves around academic politics and the shabby ways in which colleagues sometimes treat each other. If behavior among educators is part of the "hidden curriculum" presented to students, what message does it send?

6. If you were exiting that lounge and leaving your students, what would you write on the blackboard?

Chapter Six: Where Did We Go Right?

1. This chapter exercises what has been called "the Good Eye," that is, the observance of positive strengths and practices, and instances where we, as teachers, succeeded. Do you think that the exercise of the Good Eye is more or less a "feel good" indulgence or is it necessary in a teacher's improvement?

2. Reflecting on examples and practices that have worked for you as a teacher, try to list the central factors that contributed to a class or course gone surprisingly "right"?

3. This chapter highlights factors that contributed to the success of a particular course but were not the product of careful planning and deliberation. They were often the result of happenstance and momentary decision. Does this emphasis on spontaneity downplay the role of carefully honed technique? To what extent is success in teaching a matter of luck?

4. The narrator often alludes to the importance of slowing down, arguing that it is a common, contemporary mistake to believe that covering much material in a relatively short period of time accomplishes very much. Do you agree with the narrator on the benefits of slowing down in the classroom?

Chapter Seven: Two Sticks of Bare Leg

1. The author emphasizes that education is a transformative process, demanding certain conditions for its occurrence. One of these conditions is mindfulness. Would you agree? How would you define "mindfulness"? Is it similar to the author's definition?

2. The author anticipates criticism of his claim that lives depend on the mindful education he describes. He writes that some academics will argue that this assumption is "narcissistic and attributes far too much power and influence to educators." What is your position?

3. This chapter argues that there is a danger when one teaches only to the "fixity of fact" and the transfer of information. One of the author's ploys for avoiding this emphasis is showing optional, evening films, followed by popcorn and conversation. He claims that, in environments with no fixed agenda, there is often an increased chance of discovering what is on students' minds. Do you agree that it is important to engage students outside classrooms? What do these unstructured contexts provide that classrooms ordinarily don't?

4. The author claims that wonder is one of the most neglected experiences in the promotion of good teaching. What is your interpretation of wonder? Is it as necessary to teaching as this chapter maintains? How can you make room for wonder in classrooms?

5. When teaching is disconnected from human transformation, the consequences affect not only students but teachers as well. As relationships thin, teaching as an act of service becomes disparaged and resented. The author believes that the fallout even extends to teacher burnout. Is this a valid observation in your experience?

Notes

1. The original painting is on exhibit in the Royal Museum of Fine Arts in Brussels, Belgium.

2. W.H. Auden, "Musée des Beaux Arts," in *Selected Poetry of W.H. Auden* (New York: The Modern Library, 1958), 49.

3. Fyodor Dostoevsky, *The Brothers Karamazov*, trans. Constance Garnett (New York: Random House, 1996). This translation of the text appears online at www.online-literature.com/dostoevsky/brothers_karamazov.

4. Plato, *Republic*, trans. G.M.A. Grube (Indianapolis, IN: Hackett Publishing Company, 1974).

5. Ibid.

6. Unless otherwise noted, all student names are pseudonyms.

7. Grube's note is on page 168 in the 1974 Hackett edition.

8. For the link between Mnemosyne and creativity, see H. J. Rose, *Gods and Heroes of the Greeks* (New York: Meridian Books, Inc., 1958), 16-17. See also en.wikipedia.org/wiki/Mnemosyne.

9. This is the student's actual name.

10. Leon R. Kass, *The Beginning of Wisdom: Reading Genesis* (New York: Simon & Schuster, Inc., 2003), 218.

11. Darwin's translation is the Revised Standard Version of The Holy Bible.

12. I was mistakenly recalling here a line from William Carlos Williams' *Paterson* (New York: New Directions Publishing Company, 1963), which actually reads, "Were we near enough its stinking breath / would fell us" (23).

13. The quote is attributed to William Butler Yeats. See mail. goo&disp&inlins.

14. The course pairs Plato's *Republic* with Homer's *Odyssey* (trans. Robert Fitzgerald [New York: Farrar, Straus, and Giroux, 1998]); René Descartes' *Discourse on Method* (trans. Laurence J. Lafleur [New York: Macmillan Publishing Company, 1960]) with Giambattista Vico's *On the Study Methods of Our Time* (trans. Elio Gianturco [Indianapolis, IN: The Bobbs-Merrill Company, Inc., 1965]); Martha Nussbaum's *Poetic Justice* (Boston: Beacon Press, 1995) with Charles Dickens' *Hard Times* (New York: Bantam Books, 1964); and Martin Heidegger's "What are Poets For?"(In *Poetry, Language, Thought*, trans. Albert Hofstadter [New York: Harper & Row Publishers, 1971]) with William Carlos Williams' *Paterson* (New York: New Directions, 1963).

15. Dickens, *Hard Times*. The opening paragraph of *Hard Times* reads: "Now, what I want is Facts. Teach these boys and girls nothings but Facts. Facts alone are wanted in life. Plant nothing else, and root out everything else. You can only form the minds of reasoning animals upon Facts: nothing else will ever be of any service to them. . . . Stick to Facts, sir!" (1).

16. Ibid., 2.

17. Ibid., 39.

18. Ibid., 91.

19. Ibid., 1.

20. Unlike the previous pseudonyms, this student's name was Mildred: Mildred Carter.

21. Mildred Carter, "An Incredible Woman" (unpublished undergraduate paper, University of Southern Maine Department of English, 17 March 1994), 1.

22. Ibid., 2.

23. Ibid., 7-8.

24. Ibid., 8.

25. Ibid., 12-13.

26. Ibid., 13-14.

27. Michael Ende, *Momo*, trans. J. Maxwell Brownjohn (London: Penguin Books, 1984).

28. Dante Alighieri. *The Divine Comedy*, trans. Carlyle-Okey-Wicksteed (New York: Vintage Books, 1959), 11.

29. The origin of this saying is unknown. It is often included as part of Murphy's Law.

30. "Simple Gifts" was written and composed by Elder Joseph Brackett in 1848 while he was at the Shaker community in Alfred, Maine. See en.wikipedia.org/wiki/Simple_Gifts.

31. *The Producers* is a musical adapted by Mel Brooks and Thomas Meehan and based on Mel Brooks' 1968 film of the same title.

32. Aristotle, *Nicomachean Ethics*, trans. Terence Irwin (Indianapolis, IN: Hackett Publishing Company, 1985).

33. Friedrich Nietzsche, *Thus Spoke Zarathustra*, in *The Portable Nietzsche*, ed. and trans., Walter Kaufmann (New York: Viking Penguin Inc., 1982).

34. Ibid., 152.

35. *Piano Music of Friedrich Nietzsche*, John Bell Young and Constance Keene (performers), Audio CD, Newport Classics, 1992. Richard Strauss, *Also Sprach Zarathustra*, Herbert von Karajan (conductor), Berlin Philharmonic Orchestra, Audio CD, Deutsche Grammophon, 1996. *The Best of Wagner*, Eugene Ormandy, Robert Shaw (conductors), Philadelphia Orchestra and RCA Victor Orchestra, Audio CD, RCA Victor, 1991.

36. Nietzsche, *Thus Spoke Zarathustra*, 152.

37. Ibid., 146.

38. Friedrich Nietzsche, *Beyond Good and Evil*, in *Basic Writings of Nietzsche*, trans. Walter Kaufmann (New York: Random House [Modern Library], 1968), 202.

39. Ibid.

40. Nietzsche, *Thus Spoke Zarathustra*, 277.

41. Jean-Paul Sartre, *No Exit and Three Other Plays*, trans. Stuart Gilbert and I.Abel (New York: Vintage International, 1989).

42. Albert Camus, *The Myth of Sisyphus*, in *The Myth of Sisyphus and other Essays*, trans. Justin O'Brien (New York: Vintage Books, 1991).

43. Ibid., 179.

44. Ibid., 169.

45. From notes personally taken in class.

46. Ibid., 223.

47. Daryl Morazzini, "On a Philosophy *Toward* Forgiveness" (unpublished undergraduate thesis. University of Southern Maine Honors Program, May, 2002).

48. Nietzsche, *Thus Spoke Zarathustra*, 153.

49. Daryl Morazzini, unpublished undergraduate paper, University of Southern Maine Department of Philosophy, Summer 2001.

50. See, for example, Stanley Fish, "Will the Humanities Save Us?" *New York Times*, January 6, 2008.

51. Anaïs Nin, *The Winter of Artifice: A Facsimile of the Original 1939 Paris Edition* (Troy, MI: Sky Blue Press, 2007). For the quote itself, see www.quotes.net/quote/153.

52. The quote is from Henry Louis Mencken. See www.watchfuleye.com/mencken.htlm.

53. Jerome Miller, *In the Throe of Wonder: Intimations of the Sacred in a Post-Modern World* (Albany: State University of New York Press, 1992).

54. Leo Tolstoy, *The Death of Ivan Ilyich*, trans. Lynn Solotaroff (Toronto: Bantam Books, 1985).

55. Khaled Hosseini, *The Kite Runner* (New York: Riverhead Books, 2003).

56. Jean-Paul Sartre, *No Exit and Three Other Plays,* and Albert Camus, *The Plague*, trans. Stuart Gilbert (New York: Vintage International, 1991).

57. Plato, *Symposium*, trans. Alexander Nehamas and Paul Woodruff (Indianapolis, IN: Hackett Publishing Company, 1989).

58. Dostoevsky, *The Brothers Karamazov*, 60. View the text online at www.online-literature.com/dostoevsky/brothers_karamazov/9/.

59. Martha Nussbaum, *Love's Knowledge: Essays on Philosophy and Literature* (London: Oxford University Press, 1990), 46.

60. For a summary of the mythological tradition concerning Daedalus, see www.mythweb.com/encyc/entries/daedalus.html.

Permissions
and Credits

Photo: Heather Seymour

About the Author

Jeremiah Conway is a professor of Philosophy at the University of Southern Maine. He has authored over forty articles on a wide variety of topics (philosophy and literature, the nature of compassion, education and the liberal arts, and the complexities of friendship) and has won numerous awards for teaching, for example, the University of Southern Maine's Endowed Chair in Philosophy and Education, as well as the University's Outstanding Teaching Award several times. His Ph.D is from Yale University and his B.A. from Fordham University. He is a recipient of the Woodrow Wilson National Fellowship.

In addition to teaching and writing, he enjoys Irish set-dancing, keeps an old accordion warm, and likes to travel the back roads of Maine and Portugal (his wife's native turf). Having long abandoned tennis, one of his great aspirations is to beat his two sons consistently (all right, occasionally) in ping pong. He lives in Portland, Maine.

Sentient Publications, LLC publishes books on cultural creativity, experimental education, transformative spirituality, holistic health, new science, ecology, and other topics, approached from an integral viewpoint. Our authors are intensely interested in exploring the nature of life from fresh perspectives, addressing life's great questions, and fostering the full expression of the human potential. Sentient Publications' books arise from the spirit of inquiry and the richness of the inherent dialogue between writer and reader.

Our Culture Tools series is designed to give social catalyzers and cultural entrepreneurs the essential information, technology, and inspiration to forge a sustainable, creative, and compassionate world.

We are very interested in hearing from our readers. To direct suggestions or comments to us, or to be added to our mailing list, please contact:

SENTIENT PUBLICATIONS, LLC
1113 Spruce Street
Boulder, CO 80302
303-443-2188
contact@sentientpublications.com
www.sentientpublications.com